BEAM
ME UP,
JESUS

ALSO BY JIM GERARD

Celebrity Skin
Yankees Suck!

BEAM ME UP, JESUS

A
HEATHEN'S
GUIDE
TO
THE
RAPTURE

JIM GERARD

Nation Books
New York
www.nationbooks.org

BEAM ME UP, JESUS:
A Heathen's Guide to the Rapture

Copyright © 2007 Jim Gerard

AVALON
publishing group incorporated

Published by Nation Books
An Imprint of Avalon Publishing Group, Inc.
245 West 17th Street, 11th Floor
New York, NY 10011

Nation Books is a copublishing venture of the Nation Institute and
Avalon Publishing Group Incorporated.

Library of Congress Cataloging-in-Publication Data is available.

ISBN-13: 978-1-56858-327-3
ISBN-10: 1-56858-327-3

9 8 7 6 5 4 3 2 1

Interior design by Maria E. Torres
Printed in the United States of America
Distributed by Publishers Group West

The rapture (*harpazo* in Greek) is the event in certain systems of Christian eschatology (the study of the end times) in which it is stated that all born-again Christians will be taken from Earth into Heaven by Jesus Christ. While almost all forms of Christianity believe that those who are saved will have eternal life, the term *rapture* is usually applied specifically to the event in which all Christians on Earth are simultaneously transported by some manner of physical bodily ascension to join Christ.

—Wikipedia

For the Lord himself shall descend from heaven with a shout, with the voice of the archangel, and with the trump of God: and the dead in Christ shall rise first: Then we which are alive and remain shall be caught up together with them in the clouds, to meet the Lord in the air: and so shall we ever be with the Lord.

—1 Thessalonians 4:13–17

CONTENTS

CHAPTER ONE

The Rapture—A Brief Introduction

Pretend you're a Hollywood studio exec and you have a pitch meeting with a writer. He comes in and says:

> Okay, let me start with a little backstory. It's the twenty-first century, but still millions and millions of people believe in this invisible superghost who lives somewhere way, way up in space, see, and he created the entire universe and saw everything and knew everything that had ever happened or will happen— like a super-giant security camera in the sky. The people who believe in him think of him as a magic helper who protects and watches over them. It's as if

Santa Claus worked for the NSA—he sees you when you're sleeping, he knows when you're awake and engaged in possible terrorist activities and so on.

Yet, even though this ghost has, like, all the super-powers of all the superheroes rolled into one, plus other powers that no superhero has even conceived of, and he has hundreds of millions of followers, he is so insecure and possessive that he demands everyone on Earth follow him or else he condemns them to an eternity burning in a nonstop forty-hundred-alarm fire, boiling in lavalike shit and battery acid and other really fiery stuff and being constantly stabbed by devils with pitchforks. Also, two thousand years ago, he sent his only son back to Earth to redeem humanity from their wickedness by getting hung on a cross and, you know, the whole Mel Gibson treatment.

Now, here's where the story takes off: after two thousand years watching humanity slaughter itself and get really shit-faced and have wild orgies and just, like, slack off, except for a few people that invented stuff or tried to urge people to follow the superghost, the son plans to return to Earth from outer space. But before he does, he's going to beam up to Heaven all those people who believed in him, levitate them right out of their clothes, wherever they are—on an airplane, asleep, on the toilet, in *the fucking grave!* Yeah, corpses and cadavers and ghouls blasting out of the ground! It's *Saw* meets *Night of the Living Dead* with a touch of *Superman.* I mean, throngs of people filling the sky like locusts—it's an air-traffic controller's nightmare!

Meanwhile, the people left behind are just freaking out—I mean, imagine you're on this airplane going to France and suddenly the pilot just disappears! Whoa! Then you look outside and you see like hundreds of naked people whooshing up past you—I mean, we'll make most of them really bodacious babes, and then throw in an old dude going "Whoaaaa!" for laughs. And the plane just nosedives. Boom! Planes are crashing—trains, boats, computers—it's complete chaos. We see another plane, and the pilot suddenly sees all these naked flying people coming right at him, and he has to swerve to avoid them and plow! Right into the side of a mountain! Cut to a scene where this Mafia wiseguy is about to hit this guy, when the guy just flies up into the sky, and the wiseguy is like *"Maron! What the fuck?"* and he crosses himself. Huge laugh. And families are broken up and companies have to close because, like, the entire sales department just took off . . . right through the AC vent!

Anyway, nobody knows what the hell's going on! We show the news reports and CNN's blaming it on the Muslims and Fox News is blaming it on the liberals. We cut to the White House and the president is chewing out his cabinet because, like, "Is this some secret Pentagon weapon? Why wasn't I informed?" Cut to close-up of this pious secretary, and she says, "Sir, it's the Rapture." And then the president is like, "What are we going to do about it?" and some other cabinet guy goes, "There's nothing we *can* do." And the Secret Service sweeps the president away to an undisclosed location, where they fill him in on what the Rapture is.

Then we cut to our hero, Bradley Dunn. He's a physicist, and his wife used to believe in the superghost but kind of gave it up as a concession to Bradley when they got married because if it got out that she worshipped the superghost, Bradley's egghead friends would mock him, and he would never get to work on the new superparticle accelerator that's his big dream. Now she confronts him, and like a typical chick says I told you so. And she fills him in on what they're in for, and that by being such a man of science/unbeliever, he's jeopardized both of them, plus their precocious eight-year-old super-nerd son Lared—it's a combination of Jared and Larry. Never mind. But when they go into Lared's room, they find just his clothes and realize he's been Raptured, and Bradley goes to his wife, "You were teaching him all this time about the superghost?" And she's like, "Yeah," and they both realize they've lost their son, and they're happy for him but sad and scared for themselves, and it's a big, heavy drama moment where he asks her why she hasn't been Raptured and suddenly she vanishes and the audience is, like, "Was she really there and then disappeared, or was he talking to her in, like, his imagination?"

And thats only the first twenty minutes. In the rest

of the movie, the people left behind on Earth are going to suffer a seven-year nightmare of wars, plagues, attacks from supernatural creatures, asteroid collisions, and rivers of blood. . . .

Would a Hollywood studio buy that pitch? Well, maybe it would, if it was the same studio that bought *Deuce Bigalow: European Gigolo*. But most studios would've probably called security and given the writer the bum's rush before he'd even gotten to page 2.

Still, as many as a hundred million Americans believe in this story, which is known as the Rapture, a boffo scene they've extracted from the Book of Revelations, the last book of the Bible. The crazy, hallucinogenic, paranoid part. The part with the Apocalypse and its Four Horsemen, the Whore of Babylon, a seven-headed dragon, and a panoply of fantastical creatures and cataclysmic calamities straight out of *Lord of the Rings*.

Call it Gonzo Scripture.

But this book isn't for believers of the Rapture. It's for you. You know who you are. Doubter. Unbeliever. Heathen. Satanist. French-kissing liberal democrat. (If you're a Christian and have never heard about the Rapture, well, shame on you, you didn't read the Bible all the way to the end.)

If you're curious to find out what a hundred million people find so compelling about the Rapture, the nightmare that follows it called the Tribulation, and what the evangelists call "the End Times," this book will do the trick. If you're a secular humanist who believes in reason rather than magic fixers, this book will provide that warm feeling of smug superiority.

If you're a fence sitter who likes to cover all his bases, or even a closet Christian, this book will give you some practical tips on how to survive the Rapture . . . in the unlikely event that it happens and you're Left Behind.

And if you don't know into what category you fall, you can take the following Rapture IQ test. If you're the type of sinner that likes to cheat, you can skip ahead and read the complete Book of Revelation synopsis. Enjoy: the End is near!

• •

Test Your Rapture IQ

1. **The actual title of the biblical book prophesizing the Rapture is:**
    A) The Book of Revelations
    B) The Revelation of Jesus Christ . . . Unto His Servant John
    C) Jesus is Back—and This Time It's Personal
    D) Jesus: The Farewell Tour

2. Who will be revealed as the Antichrist?
    A) Tom Cruise
    B) Osama Bin Laden
    C) Simon Cowell
    D) O.J.

3. Which people will be Raptured?
    A) All Christians
    B) Only those Christians who have taken Jesus into their hearts
    C) Christians and non-Christians who are married to Christians
    D) Christians and non-Christians represented by Alan Dershowitz

4. The Tribulation refers to:
- A) A seven-year period of time that roughly coincides with the Rapture, in which believers will experience worldwide persecution
- B) The eternal damnation of sinners
- C) A Christian thrash-metal band
- D) Being locked in a closet for twenty-four hours with Dick Vitale

5. When the Rapture occurs, what will the government do?
- A) Pass a bill making the Rapture illegal
- B) Levy a Rapture tax on all assets Left Behind
- C) Launch a massive PR campaign denying that the Rapture is taking place
- D) Let Michael Brown handle it

6. What will likely happen to those people Left Behind?
- A) They will die a slow, miserable, terrified death, tormented by their estrangement from the Lord and ultimately eaten by carnivorous giant slugs or some other crazy shit we've never seen before, unless they repent and take Jesus into their hearts, in which case they'll get eaten by carnivorous giant slugs and then spend the rest of eternity next to God in Heaven.
- B) They will form a new utopian society of smart people.
- C) They will compete in the *Left Behind* reality series.
- D) They will suffer from low self-esteem and need lots of therapy.

7. What awaits the Raptured in Heaven?
- A) A seat at their Lord's side
- B) Eternal joy
- C) A gold watch and a perfunctory speech by Jesus thanking them for their service to the company
- D) Disappointment, because it doesn't measure up to Leisure Village

8. The Mark of the Beast is
   A) A footprint left by Sasquatch
   B) A post-Rapture identifying mark that Satan will force everyone
   on Earth to accept in order to buy or sell anything
   C) Also known as cat-scratch fever
   D) A yellow stain left on your couch

9. Of the following personages, who does not appear in the Book of Revelation?
   A) God
   B) Satan
   C) The Antichrist
   D) Al Roker

10. Armageddon is
   A) The name of the epic battle between the forces of Jesus and the
   forces of Satan that takes place during the End Times
   B) A 1998 film in which Ben Affleck saved the Earth from an
   asteroid collision to a soundtrack by Aerosmith
   C) A toilet-bowl cleaner
   D) All of the above

Answers

1. B. The book was revealed to an early Christian named John on the island of Patmos sometime in the first century a.d. Scholars disagree about whether this John also wrote the Gospel of John, the Epistles of John, or the to-do list of John. Some contend that one person wrote everything, others believe there were three different Johns, and one scholar believes that the author was a man with three different personalities, all named John.

2. C. Simon Cowell. And his first words will be: "You're the worst humans I've ever seen!"

3. D. When dealing with the Old Testament god, it doesn't hurt to have a Jewish lawyer.

4. A, C, and D. (*Note:* The Tribulation is a Christian metal band whose biggest hit is "Bend Over, Satan, I Am Thy Master!")

5. C. According to some Rapturologists, the one-world government will try to reassure the public that the asteroids striking the earth, the plagues of flying serpents, and the levitation of millions of Christians into the Heavens are nothing to worry about. The head of the one-world government will announce, "Go shopping—or else Jesus wins."

6. A. Either way, their souls will suffer such anguish of separation from Jesus that they will beg for the giant slug to eat them. If the giant slug they happen to come across is full or on the Master Cleanse or for whatever other reason can't eat them immediately, they will keep going until they find one that can.

7. A. Yes, but the only people to actually sit at Jesus' side will be those few fortunate souls with a luxury box, from which they can watch the heathen die of war and pestilence. Due to restricted space in Heaven, most of the Raptured will be seated very far away from the action, and some will only have a partial view of Armageddon.

8. B. The various Rapturologist factions disagree on many things, such as exactly when the Rapture is coming and whether the Tribulation will occur before, during, or after the Rapture. But there's one thing upon which they all agree: don't take the mark of the beast! It's the Antichrist's driver's license, a sinister ID bracelet, and a Satanic tattoo all rolled into one. Since, however, you will not be able to conduct any commercial transactions without it, those who refuse it will basically be reduced to bartering their old eight-track tapes of Foghat for food and shelter. The price of eternal salvation is steep, my friend.

9. D. Although he does make a cameo in the Book of Genesis, standing before a weather map and saying to Noah, "I told you a low-pressure area was coming through."

10. D. All of the above.

Scoring

8-10: Make your Rapture reservations. You're going first class.

6-7: Let us know how it feels to be Raptured by UPS.

4-5: The Rapture Nazi says, "No Rapture for you."

2-3: You won't even be allowed to watch it on television.

0-1: Jesus hates you.

CHAPTER TWO

The Book of Revelation— Reader's Digest Version

Although references to the Rapture and the "End Times" are found in other books of the Bible, such as Daniel, Ezekiel, Thessalonians, and the Gospel of Matthew, their primary rendering occurs in the book of Revelation.

This book comes from a long line of apocalyptic literature. Other examples are the book of Isaiah, the book of Daniel and the New York Knicks' media guide.

The main theme of the Book of Revelation is the wrath of God, which is so much worse than the wrath of Khan, it's not funny. In fact, some contemporary scholars have tallied the number of deaths during the End Times prophesied in Revelation and prorated it to the Earth's current population. The final tally: five billion. Of course, most of the victims will be sinners, with a few innocent bystanders who happened to be in the wrong place at the wrong time. As God says, "Shit happens."

To boil down Revelation, it's God going postal on the unrepentant and an awful wicked beast ruling the whole world while flipping God the bird.

Lastly, it's about Jesus, the avenging bloodthirsty warrior with a sword. As Revelation says, "He will rule the nations with a rod of iron, as a potter strikes a pot with iron and it just completely shatters."

Make no mistake: this is not good, liberal Jesus. This is bad, neocon Jesus.

Most modern interpreters believe that Revelation was written sometime during the reign of the Roman emperor Domitian (81–96 C.E.), by one of three people named John: John the Apostle, John the Evangelist, or another guy named John, who had been exiled to the island of Patmos. (One radical theologian believes it was written by five guys named Moe.)

Whoever the author was, he addressed Revelation to seven Christian communities who had scattered from Jerusalem to what is now Turkey to avoid Roman persecution. This was prudent, since if they ended up staying there was a good chance that they could end up being the stars of a Coliseum event that ended with the announcement, "No lions were harmed in the preceding performance."

It wasn't until the fifth century C.E. that the Bible as we know it was fully codified. Before then, various factions conspired to have their favorite material included, while texts that portrayed Jesus in a way that didn't conform to the church's carefully propagated image of him were expunged. Those stray biblical runners-up are known as Apocrypha, the remain-dered titles of their time.

BOOKS THAT ALMOST MADE IT INTO THE BIBLE

- *The Book of Rants*

- *Caesar's Way*–the Roman emperors Julius and Augustus tell you how to train your dog

- *I Feel Bad about My Neck* (by Barabbas)

- *The World Is Flat . . . Literally*

- *Tuesdays with Diocletian*

- *What Color Is Your Chariot?*

- *The Joys of Yiddish*

- *Natural Cures Hippocrates Doesn't Want You to Know About*

- *Caligula's Just Not That Into You*

- *Who Moved Thy Cheese?*

- *Rome Sucks,* by Noam Chomsky the Elder

- *Apostles Twelve* (the sequel to Apostles Eleven in which Jesus and his rowdy band of swingin' acolytes pull off the biggest palace heist in the history of Rome)

Almost from its inception, Revelation stirred controversy within the early church. In the fourth century, St. John Chrysostom and other bishops argued against including it in

the New Testament canon, chiefly because of the difficulties
of interpreting its whacked-out symbolism and the danger
that people would use it to justify all kinds of irrational beliefs.

Even then, they knew.

Because the Book of Revelation is slow going, and because
I don't want to run afoul of copyright laws (many modern
translations of the Bible are copyrighted, and Jesus doesn't
get one penny in royalties), I will spare you the chore of
plowing through the entire book. Instead, I have provided a
crib notes version. (*Disclaimer:* Cribbing is a sin.)

Chapter 1: Jesus appears to John with greetings from the
Father. The Son of God apparently has aged since his last biblical appearance, for His hair is "white like snow." (Crucifixion
will do that to you.) In fact, he refers to himself as the "firstborn of the dead," which is like calling yourself the world's
slimmest fatso. Somewhat ominously, he tells John that he
holds the keys to the underworld, you know, just in case John
gets any funny ideas about sinning.

John also describes Jesus as wearing a golden girdle and
seven golden candlesticks, an entrance that anticipates Lib-
erace by two millennia. Then Jesus shoots knives out of his
mouth—a reverse-sword swallowing act that hasn't been
equaled in the annals of Vegas.

Finally, Jesus asks John to take down the message he has for
the seven churches. Or, as *The Idiot's Guide to the Book of
Revelation*—a tome that truly knows its audience—puts it:
"Seven churches get a performance review." This analogy only
goes so far; unlike in Revelation, a bad performance review
doesn't usually result in the employee being eaten by a dragon,
one of the many trippily horrific things that happens during
the Tribulation (but more about that later in the book).

Chapter 2: Jesus tells John that as much as he respects the hard work put in by the leaders of the church in Ephesus, they are still considered fallen because, among other transgressions, they've given a prophetess named Jezebel "the space to commit fornication" and to "teach and seduce His servants" to do likewise. He insists that from now on they teach all the Jezebels abstinence instead of sex ed.

Jesus begrudgingly credits the Ephesians with hating the Nicolaitans as much as He does—a big point in the Ephesians' favor, for if there's one thing we learn about Revelation Jesus it's that deep down, beneath all the turn-the-other-cheek-advising and Beatitude-bestowing, the guy is a *huge* hater. (The Nicolaitans were a sect in Asia Minor who Jesus said led lives "of unrestrained indulgence.")

Jesus castigates those who claim to be Jews but actually "are the synagogue of Satan," which is a Reform sect based in Beverly Hills. He tells John, "Behold, the devil is about to cast some of you into prison, that ye may be tried; and ye shall have tribulation ten days. Be thou faithful unto death, and I will give thee the crown of life." (On the other hand, the sentence Satan hands out is *only* ten days, and it's possible you could get it knocked down to community service—you know, keeping the sodomites in line with a pitchfork three hours day.)

Continuing his rant, Jesus promises to cast Jezebel into a bed along with her adulterer-lovers and send them, bed and all, "into great tribulation," and then put it on pay-per-view.

Jesus adds, "I will kill her children with death," sounding like Conan the Barbarian.

Chapter 3: Jesus continues raving in the same vein against the rest of the seven churches. He warns them all to stick to the straight and narrow, or else, "I shalt come on thee as a thief, and thou shalt not know what hour I will come upon thee." He also threatens to "spue thee out of my mouth" and to "blot his name out in the book of life" Yikes! Who's talking here—Jesus or Paulie Walnuts?

Chapter 4: As Jesus finishes up his rant, a door to Heaven opens, and John hears a voice "like a trumpet talking" that urges him to rise up to Heaven, where he will be shown the future of mankind—the world's longest war movie.

In Heaven, John sees the Lord sitting on a throne surrounded by a rainbow, twenty-four elders wearing golden crowns and four beasts full of eyes "before and behind. The first beast was like a lion, the second like a calf, the third had a face as a man and the fourth was like a flying eagle." All the creatures praise the Lord and Industrial Light and Magic.

Chapter 5: John tells of a book lying near the throne, "sealed with seven seals." (What's with the redundancies? The Lord created the world in six days, but he couldn't find a decent copy editor?) This book is so heavy or powerful or something that it can't be opened by anyone—until a lamb with seven horns and seven eyes deigns to crack it. The lamb turns out to be Jesus, and hundreds of thousands of angels sing his praises and worship Him in a scene that resembles a National Socialist rally from Nuremberg in the thirties.

Chapter 6: The first four seals are opened, and they reveal four different-colored horses. The fourth, pale horse is Death. One of the horses utters, "A measure of wheat for a penny, and three measures of barley for a penny; and see thou hurt not the oil and the wine," which makes no sense, but is more impressive than anything Mr. Ed ever said. The opening of the fifth seal reveals the souls of all the persecuted and martyred

Christians, whose hunger for payback on those still living on Earth is . . . well, perhaps you have caught Charles Bronson in *Death Wish?* About ten times as seething.

Things really go haywire when they pop the sixth seal. An earthquake strikes, the sun turns black and the moon bloody, the stars of Heaven fall on the earth, every mountain and island is uprooted, and, in response, the entire population of Earth . . . hides themselves in their dens. Yes, the day of wrath has arrived, and the sinners are watching *Celebrity Poker.* So typical of the fallen, isn't it? But then they fully realize what's happening and start begging the mountains to fall on them and hide them from the face of "the wrath of the lamb." (*Note:* This title, "Wrath of the Lamb," test-marketed in the toilet.)

Chapter 7: Four angels appear, one at each corner of the world, whose job it is to "hurt the earth and the sea." To make sure they get it right, they hire Halliburton. A fifth angel appears and bestows God's seal on the forehead of the faithful, the number 144,000 (twelve thousand from each of the twelve tribes of Israel).

The 144,000 are said to be, "These . . . which came out of great tribulation, and have washed their robes, and made them white in the blood of the Lamb." To this day, no one knows how washing robes in blood will bleach them white, because the formula is a secret. The robe washers excessively flatter the Lord, who has even more sycophants than Martha Stewart.

Chapter 8: The seventh seal is opened. The angels trash the Earth like a British rock band at the penthouse suite at the Hyatt on Sunset Boulevard. Fire, thunder, earthquakes, a burning mountain, a star named Wormwood, and a whole bunch of laser disks and other stuff they had lying around their attic are dumped on our planet. Plus the sun and the moon are dimmed. A talking eagle flies overhead and quips something to the effect of "If you think *this* is bad, wait till you see what else the Lord has in store for you."

Just what we need, after being burned out of our homes and drowning in a river of blood—a wisecracking bird.

Chapter 9: Okay. Imagine that the Book of Revelation is a blockbuster movie—and while Mel Gibson is alive you can't ever discount the possibility. You're sitting in the theater, and you watch the following depicted in full CGI-Dolby glory:

> And out of the smoke came forth locusts upon the earth; and power was given them, as the scorpions of the earth have power. And it was said unto them that they should not hurt the grass of the earth, neither any green thing, neither any tree, but only such men as have not the seal of God on their foreheads. And it was given them that they should not kill them, but that they should be tormented five months: and their torment was as the torment of a scorpion, when it striketh a man. . . . And the shapes of the locusts were like unto horses prepared for war; and upon their heads as it were crowns like unto gold, and their faces were as men's faces. And they had hair as the hair of women, and their teeth were as teeth of lions. And they had breastplates, as it were breastplates of iron; and the sound of their wings was as the sound of chariots, of many horses rushing to war. And they have tails like unto scorpions, and stings; and in their tails is their power to hurt men five months.

This—this is the part where the stoned couple sitting next to you in matching unisex Phat Farm ensembles, who have been making out, noisily chomping Goobers, checking their cell-phone text messages, giggling to each other and talking trash to the characters on the screen, oblivious to everyone else in the theater, would—mouths agape—shout, "This is whack shit!"

And it gets even whacker. Four angels are charged with killing one-third of all men. Hell's angels? I think yes.

Despite all this hallucinatory carnage, the survivors on Earth "repented not of their murders, nor of their sorceries, nor of their fornication, nor of their thefts." Yet more proof that the death penalty isn't a deterrent.

Chapter 10: Seven thunders start to talk, and John gets ready to take notes. A voice from Heaven tells him to put away his notebook and instead eat a book that an angel is holding in his hand. John is told to "prophecy over many peoples and nations and tongues and kings" while wondering how he's going to explain this whole thing to his gastroenterologist.

Chapter 11: Jesus reveals that the two candlesticks are actually his "witnesses" who have incredible powers: they can keep the skies from raining, turn rivers into blood and so on, and yet . . . they're defenseless against a beast that will emerge from "the bottomless pit" (which theologians have traced to the kitchen at Denny's). This is the first mention of *the* beast, whose mark will become a more famous brand than Prada. Some Christian fundamentalists, like Pat Robertson, believe that the Beast is Hugo Chavez. Others think it's Michael Kinsley.

God sets off an earthquake that kills seven thousand. And there's no benefit concert.

Chapter 12: A pregnant woman goes into labor. A dragon

awaits the delivery, so it can devour the child as soon as it emerges from the womb. (And Jerry Falwell thinks Hollywood is depraved?) Instead, the child is whisked up to Heaven, where a war happens to be going on between Michael the Archangel and his band of brothers and that same dragon, which is subsequently referred to as a serpent (aka Satan). The dragon is hurled back to Earth and tries to drown the woman who just delivered, but Heavenly forces protect her.

I know what you're thinking: *where can I cop some of the 'shrooms John took?*

Chapter 13: John sees a beast rise up out of the sea with seven heads, ten horns, and ten crowns. (It isn't clear how the horns are divided, but it's obvious some of the heads have gotten short-changed.) Upon the heads is stamped "the name of blasphemy."

John continues, "And the beast which I saw was like unto a leopard, and his feet were as the feet of a bear, and his mouth as . . . a lion." The beast then began "speaking great things and blasphemies."

Some of the beast's blasphemies included:

- Jesus sucks cocks in Hell.
- Don't let Him kid you. The Lord is Botoxed to the gills.
- Satan will refinance your mortgage at a rock-bottom price.
- There are no public toilets in Heaven.
- That *DaVinci Code*? All true.

The beast is given power over all nations and charged with making war with the saints.

Finally, we come to the introduction of the mark of the beast. . . .

> And he causeth all, both small and great, rich and poor, free and bond, to receive a mark in their right hand, or in their foreheads. And that no man might buy or sell, save he that had the mark, or the name of the beast, or the number of his name. . . . And his number is Six hundred threescore and six.

Remember: you can only have the mark of the beast on your right hand or forehead. Do not—I repeat—do not have it tattooed on your ass. Satan will be pissed.

Chapter 14: God and his 144,000* "sealed" or chosen ones stand on Mt. Zion and listen to the voice of Heaven and thunder and "harpers harping with their harps." Regular harps, not Jew's harps.

It turns out that the chosen ones are virgins (Is it me, or is this starting to sound like some Jim Jones suicide cult?) Angels—God's flunkies—appear and sing His praises. One of the angels puts a city under some sort of cosmic winepress, "and blood came out . . . even unto the horse bridles, by the space of a thousand and six hundred furlongs." And it had top notes of sage, elderberry, and human.

Chapter 15: One of the beasts gives seven angels—who are already carrying seven plagues—seven vials full of the wrath of

---

*A word about the number 144,000, which is mentioned several times in Revelation: the Rapture-lovers perceive these as two separate groups of 144,000, one group of which will be Raptured and the other, chosen from the twelve tribes of Israel, will be Left Behind and evangelize after the Rapture.

God. The temple is closed until the plagues are fulfilled. The Jews petition the Lord for the name of a good Chinese restaurant. The Lord replies, "One Hung Lo." The Jews crack up, and God slaughters them. The Christians, who don't find the punch line funny—in fact, don't even get it—decide to convert One Hung Lo, the owner of the restaurant, and are saved. One Hung Lo later abandons the faith and ends up as the butt of more crude ethnic jokes, including the immortal one about the Chinese man asking his bride on their wedding night if they could do "number 69," and the bride responding, "You mean beef wiff bloccoli?"

Chapter 16: Kings from the East are gathered together in preparation for a mammoth war on a plain called Armageddon.

The first angel pours his vial onto the earth and creates some kind of smallpox epidemic. The second angel pours his into the sea, and "it became as the blood of a dead man: and every living soul died in the sea." There are rivers and oceans of blood, which are drunk by saints, frogs pour out of the mouths of dragons, cities are destroyed by Perfect Hailstorms. . . . My head is spinning from all this holy vengeance and surreal violence. Why don't we take a break and review some of the other great titles and gift items from Nation Books?

- *How to Pick Up Chicks* by Michael Dukakis
- *We're Mad as Hell and We're Going to Write Some Letters to the Editor: A Primer for Taking Back America* by the Democratic Leadership Council
- *The Zapatista Diet* by Subcommandante Marcos
- *How to Strip for Your Man* by Barbara Boxer
- *An African-American, a Differently Abled*

Person, a Transgendered Person, and an Inuit Go into a Bar: 1,001 Politically Correct Jokes for Any Occasion by the University of California at Berkeley Sociology Department
- *My Life in the Ring* by Markos Moulitsas
- No Logo™ T-shirts, coffee mugs, boxer briefs, and tote bags. (No Logo™ is a division of No Logo, Inc., including Baby No Logo and Absolutely No Logo.)

Chapter 17: In this chapter, John is dragged by an angel to see the famous Whore of Babylon. She "sits upon a scarlet colored beast, full of names of blasphemy, having seven heads and ten horns," and on her forehead are written the words: MYSTERY, BABYLON THE GREAT, THE MOTHER OF HARLOTS AND ABOMINATIONS OF THE EARTH. (Before that, her forehead displayed a fast-food ad featuring an animated chicken that waved at passersby.)

Chapter 18: An angel warns everyone to stay away from Babylon. It has "become the habitation of devils, and the hold of every foul spirit, and a cage of every unclean and hateful bird. . . . Her plagues come in one day, death, and mourning, and famine; and she shall be utterly burned with fire." Needless to say, this kills tourism.

In the next sentence, John switches tenses and tells us Babylon has been destroyed. Go figure.

Chapter 19: Let's go to the highlights:

- The marriage of the lamb is announced (although the bride's name is withheld out of respect for her family).

- "The voice of a great multitude" sings the Lord's praises and presents him with a commemorative plaque.
- The Lord leads an army on white horses with which to smite the nations.
- The beast and the false prophet—a great name for a pro-wrestling tag team—are burned.
- "He hath on his vesture and on his thigh a name written, KING OF KINGS, AND LORD OF LORDS." Like we didn't know? This guy acts more like the Donald than the Creator.
- An angel standing in the sun invites "all the fowls that fly in the midst of Heaven" to the "supper of the great God, that ye may eat the flesh of all men, both free and bond, both small and great." Hitchcock would later steal this idea for *The Birds*.
- The beast and the Antichrist are thrust into a pit of fire and brimstone, slow cooked, and served at Tony Roma's.

Chapter 20: Satan is also tossed into the fire pit and told that he's up for parole in a thousand years. His attorney plea-bargains the sentence down to nine hundred. After Satan is "loosed out of his prison," the first thing he does is "deceive the nations which are in the four quarters of the earth, Gog, and Magog, to gather them together to battle."

It's so hard to stay straight.

Alas, crime doesn't pay, so Satan is picked up and tossed back into the pit, "where [he] shall be tormented day and night" by being forced to listen to heretics talk on their cell phones for the rest of eternity.

Then the other sinners are lined up for the Last Judgment. If that's not bad enough, their fates are going to be voted on by a TV audience.

Chapter 21: The holy city, New Jerusalem, descends from Heaven. A voice declares that "God shall wipe away all tears from their eyes; and there shall be no more death, neither sorrow, nor crying, neither shall there be any more pain."

Not only that, but you can eat as much cheesecake as you want without gaining weight.

The Lord promises the godly that they will "inherit all things." And just in case "the fearful, and unbelieving, and the abominable, and murderers, and whoremongers, and sorcerers, and idolaters, and all liars" haven't yet gotten the message, they "shall have their part in the lake which burneth with fire and brimstone: which is the second death." (The first death is doing dinner theater with Tony Danza.)

The angel finally shows John the Lamb's wife. It is the city of Jerusalem.

Then comes Jerusalem's Al Gore moment: The city "had no need of the sun, neither of the moon, to shine in it," for it is powered totally by self-righteousness.

Chapter 22: In this final chapter of Revelation, John promises to love, honor, and obey the Lord, who in turn lays down the law yet one more time: believe and be saved; be caught with a copy of *Inches* magazine and be damned.

So, while the overt lesson from Revelation is that good triumphs over evil, there is a caveat.

At the very end of the last chapter of Revelation, the Lord says something that every believer in the Rapture should read with great trepidation: "For I testify unto every man that heareth the words of the prophecy of this book, *If any man shall add unto these things, God shall add unto him the plagues that are written in this book.*"

To wit, don't go running off using the Book of Revelation to justify everything from the invasion of Iran to the creation of an American theocracy.

And yes, the sound you just heard was Pat Robertson going, "Uh-oh . . ."

That's right. Nowhere in Revelation is there any mention of the Rapture. The most explicit reference to the Rapture—as well as an allusion to the Second Coming—occurs in Matt. 24:29–31:

> [29] Immediately after the tribulation of those days shall the sun be darkened, and the moon shall not give her light, and the stars shall fall from heaven, and the powers of the heavens shall be shaken:
>
> [30] And then shall appear the sign of the Son of man in heaven: and then shall all the tribes of the earth mourn, and they shall see the Son of man coming in the clouds of heaven with power and great glory.
>
> [31] And he shall send his angels with a great sound of a trumpet, and they shall gather together his elect from the four winds, from one end of heaven to the other.

As you can see, Matthew says that the Rapture will occur after the Tribulation, and seemingly in combination with the Resurrection—God's multitasking. It's not understood how the current popular interpretation of the Rapture—as an event that precedes Armageddon, the Resurrection and the End Times—evolved, but it has been the official line since the time of the early church fathers. Then again, these are the same people who furiously debated how many angels could dance on the head of a pin; then, when they got frustrated that they couldn't arrive at an answer, started killing Jews.

CHAPTER THREE

Whose Rapture Is It, Anyway?

The Book of Revelation entered the Bible as we know now it in the first century C.E. Most scholars think it was around the year 95.

Ever since, the legitimacy of Revelation and the Rapture as Scripture has been in dispute. The early Christian fathers were ambivalent about including it in the Bible. Martin Luther had no use for it (and was said to doodle on it). The Eastern Orthodox Church omits it from their Divine Liturgy, the only book of the Bible to suffer that ignominy. Dan Brown swears it's a Vatican conspiracy to demonize Satan, who he says is misunderstood and the victim of a broken home.

The biggest point of contention is between those who interpret Revelation as a symbolic attempt by church fathers to maintain control over their satellites in a fragmented Christian community, and those who believe that the book should be taken literally as a prophecy of the "End Times" (and who have been inhaling from a can of Sterno).

Because Revelation is so symbol heavy, it has spawned a religious subgenre: Rapture handicapping, you might call it. There are three main schools that claim to know exactly when the Rapture will occur, and numerous lesser ones. (See box: Lesser-Known Predictions of When the Rapture Will Occur.)

Below is a brief summary of the various interpretations, which I have compiled after immersing myself in the foremost biblical scholarship, especially *The Complete Idiot's Guide to the Book of Revelation*. (This book establishes its academic legitimacy by using text boxes with headings such as "Apoca-lips now," accompanied by an animated Bible with a pair of smiling lips. Trust me: if you see your Bible smiling at you, it's time to get off the sauce.)

MAJOR SCHOOLS OF RAPTURE INTERPRETATION

The biblical prophecy school believes that Revelation, when interpreted in conjunction with the Book of Daniel and other sections of the Bible, constitutes a prophecy of the end of the world. (*Source:* Wikipedia) Most of these people are evangelical Christians who believe that the Rapture is a literal event—with first the dead Christians, then, in short order, the live ones Sputniking into space—and that all of history is just a trailer.

A subgroup of believers subscribe to what's known as the Preterist, or historicist, view: that the Book of Revelation prophesized events that happened in the first century. In order for this to work, Revelation had to have been written in 68 C.E. Any later, and it would be predicting events that already happened. Which is like John Madden boasting, "I've got the winners of last Sunday's NFL games!"

But most people who believe that the Rapture is biblical prophecy are futurists—meaning that they're sure that the End Times will occur in the future, and within their lifetimes. It's vanity religion, practiced by the same personality type who believes that in a past life, she was Joan of Arc and not Joan of Newark.

Futurist interpretations generally predict a Great Tribulation, a seven-year period when believers will experience worldwide persecution—that is, when their assault rifles will be confiscated. This will be followed by a resurrection of the dead and a Rapture of the Christians into Heaven at the same time as the Second Coming, or when God/Christ begins his thousand-year reign on Earth. This last bit makes no sense; God whisks the Christians away just as the party is starting? Talk about being damned if you do and damned if you don't.

But the Tribulationists can't even agree among themselves. These cosmic nitpickers include pre-Tribulationists (those who believe the Rapture will come before the Tribulation), mid-Tribulationists (during the Trib), and post-Tribulationists (after the Trib). So remember: if you go into a bar in Kansas and someone brings up the Tribulation, just change the subject.

Another view of the pre-Trib people is delineated by the collective wisdom of Wikipedia:

> [Pre-Tribulation] is the belief that the Rapture will occur at the beginning of the 70th Week of Daniel, the final seven years of this age. Christian believers will be translated into immortal bodies in the Rapture before the great persecutions by the Antichrist as he comes into his Beast role midway through the final seven years. . . . As soon as the Rapture occurs

(according to this doctrine), many others will believe
in the Jesus Christ of the Bible and will be saved, even
though they missed the "rapture" and will now have
to go through that tribulation period with everyone
else on the Earth. When those people become new
Christians, they will be part of "the Church" on earth
during this time period. They will witness during the
first three-and-one-half years, and they will also witness during the last three and a half years, or 1260
days of the Great Tribulation, which follow.

I know: this is even harder to figure out than Bush's Medicaid
prescription drug plan.

And that's even before we factor in the post-Tribulationists,
who believe that the Rapture will occur after the Tribulation.
This means that during the seven years of mayhem, when God
and the Devil have a cosmological steel-cage match, the chosen
stay behind along with the fallen, cheering God on and even
doing the wave.

According to the historicists, Revelation predicts that the
church will gradually conquer the whole world, yet somehow
end up a persecuted minority. (You'd think this would be an
almost impossible trick, but after backing the Germans in World
War II and launching the current child-molestation epidemic,
would you bet against it?)

The historicists also believe that the Second Coming will
occur when the forces of the Antichrist—aka the European
Union—go to war against Israel.

Lastly, there is the historo-critical interpretation—that Revelation is a symbolic text delivered by church fathers to scare
wayward Christians who had begun to harbor heretical beliefs,

invent pseudo-Christian practices, and distort Jesus' teachings. (See box: Early Christian Heresies; and Box: Miracles Falsely Attributed to Jesus.)

As you know, the futurists have held the predominant view throughout history, never more so than today, when the idea of the Rapture as a literal event permeates pop culture—there are Rapture T-shirts, bumper stickers, books, and videos. It's a veritable industry, as we shall see in the next chapter.

EARLY CHRISTIAN HERESIES

- Adam and Steve

- The Last Supper was "All-U-Can-Eat."

- Jesus Christ, Superstar

- Screw the meek.

- Jesus charged for miracles

- The Ten Highly Effective Commandments of Powerful Christians

- Satan tempted Jesus with all the kingdoms of the earth, then asked, "Deal or no deal?"

- Render to Caesar what is Caesar's, and also wear a Caesar haircut.

- Thou must doeth the Funky Chicken.

- Converts baptized in a dunk tank

- After the cry "Give us Barabbas!" Jesus tells jeering Roman crowd to "buzz off."

MIRACLES FALSELY ATTRIBUTED TO JESUS

- Changes water into Bud Lite
- Escapes from locked safe while underwater
- Bench-presses a Buick
- Uses X-ray vision to look right through Pilate's robe
- Does chariot wheelie
- Makes the ace of spades pop out of Judas's ear
- Moonwalks on water
- Saws a Philistine in half and leaves him that way
- Doesn't heal leper, but offers to sign him up with an HMO
- Throws a no-hitter in an apostalic beer-league softball game

LESSER-KNOWN PREDICTIONS OF WHEN THE RAPTURE WILL OCCUR

- During halftime of this year's Super Bowl, right after the Southern California high school drill teams and dancers, who many people will blame for the Apocalypse
- April 1, 2025. The doomed will think it's an April Fool's prank, and the saved will float up to Heaven while derisively pointing the finger of a giant foam hand at those Left Behind.
- During an episode of *The Flavor of Love*
- When your back is turned
- The day before this book is published—just my luck

THE END IS NEAR (NO, THIS TIME HE REALLY MEANS IT)
An editorial by Harvey Saperstein, the atheist insult comic

Killer hurricanes. Earthquakes. Bird flu pandemic. Monster tornadoes. These catastrophes can only mean one thing—Beam Me Up, Jesus! All this death and destruction, and the End Times people couldn't be happier. The Messiah is finally going to return.

Now, it doesn't matter that these same people have been predicting the end of the world for the centuries. No, Christ is coming back—and this time he's loaded for bear.

But should we believe these prophets of doom? They've been wrong for two thousand years. They predicted Jesus would return when the vandals sacked Rome. When the plague ravaged Europe. Whenever there was a big war or some global calamity, Jesus was expected to blow into town. Like it took something really huge to get his attention. Like he's got ADD.

In reality, he responds to disasters even slower than FEMA.

What does it take to get this guy off his duff? And why does he always cancel at the last minute? Did he get a better offer? Is his To-Do list that long? Get him a PDA!

"November 28th, 1:45 P.M., End Times."

If you ask me, this Jesus guy is just totally unreliable. And not only that. The end-timers say that Jesus will *only* come back during a time of tribulation, and he'll *only* show up in the Holy Land, and *only* after the Jews have returned there, but there has to be a certain number of Christians there, too. I mean, this guy's got more demands than J-Lo.

People who believe in the Rapture say that when Jesus finally comes back, the heathens are going to be left behind while Christians are going to be beamed up into Heaven, instantaneously, wherever they are. Raptured right out of their clothes. Yeah, God doesn't do laundry.

In a way, I feel sorry for the end-timers. I mean, they're always waiting to be Raptured and always disappointed. I mean, what if you gave away your house to a heathen cousin? That's got to be embarrassing.

Christian: "Um, could I have my house back?" "

Heathen Cousin: "Don't tell me—Jesus stood you up again?"

Christian: "No, no, it was a scheduling mix-up. Just get out of my damn house."

Until the Rapture comes, the true believers are going to have to settle for a Christian theme park. I'm not kidding. There are already a bunch of them. Sure, you can be saved. But the lines! And no picture-taking during the Last Judgment.

Good night. You've been a really heathen audience.

TOP TEN EXCUSES FOR
WHY JESUS HAS NOT COME AGAIN

*By People through the Ages Who Made
Bold Predictions That He Would*

1. "My sundial stopped."

2. "The dog ate my prediction."

3. "He's got other things on his mind."

4. "I said He would come today—give or take two thousand years."

5. "Jesus? Oh, He was just here. You just missed him."

6. "The world ended in 1865. This is just a hallucination."

7. "He wants it to be a surprise."

8. "He's on a book tour."

9. "It's not you—it's Him."

10. "Oh, I didn't mean *that* Jesus."

ESSAY QUESTION: HOW THE BOOK OF REVELATION STACKS UP AGAINST RANDOMLY GENERATED SPAM

In 250 words or less, compare and contrast the following excerpt from the Book of Revelation and a randomly generated piece of spam. Hint: There is no right answer.

BOOK OF REVELATION

The beast that thou sawest was, and is not; and shall ascend out of the bottomless pit, and go into perdition: and they that dwell on the earth shall wonder, whose names were not written in the book of life from the foundation of the world, when they behold the beast that was, and is not, and yet is. And here is the mind which hath wisdom. The seven heads are seven mountains, on which the woman sitteth. And there are seven kings: five are fallen, and one is, and the other is not yet come; and when he cometh, he must continue a short space. And the beast that was, and is not, even he is the eighth, and is of the seven, and goeth into perdition.

RANDOMLY GENERATED SPAM

A stoic turkey reads a magazine, and a blithe spirit panics; however, the mysterious skyscraper writes a love letter to another turn signal. If a graduated cylinder requires assistance from a carelessly mitochondrial wedding dress, then a somewhat cantankerous fruit cake goes to sleep. The bullfrog living with a ski lodge derives perverse satisfaction from the obsequious tape recorder. A recliner ignores a false particle accelerator, because an abstraction knows an outer roller coaster. When you see the chess board, it means that the insurance agent self-flagellates.

CHAPTER FOUR

The Rapture in Pop Culture

A Google search for the word *rapture* turned up 3,120,000 results. Even considering that about half of these were Web pages devoted to the Viking heavy-metal band of the same name, that's still . . . far too many.

The Rapture's first pop-culture appearance seems to have been in a 1941 propaganda film of the same name. Made with scissors, paste, odd bits of stock film (the ocean tossing, a baby in a crib, a man looking incredulously at his bloody hands) that were hoary in Edison's day, an opening theme ripped off from the radio crime show *The Shadow,* and a portentous tone of muted hysteria, the film could easily be called *Rapture Madness.*

The film was part of a series called The Scriptures Visualized, and its shaky, faded images, tinny soundtrack, and wooden narrator are reminiscent of the educational films they showed us in grade school, like *Our Friend the Paramecium*.

It begins with the narrator intoning, "Someday soon, in a moment, in the twinkling of the eye, life will be suddenly changed for all of us. Events unspeakably strange and startling will occur with amazing rapidity. Speeding trains will plunge unsuspecting passengers into a black eternity as Christian engineers are plucked from the throttle. . . ."

Cut to a shot of two trains in a head-on collision.

A close-up of medical instruments falling out of someone's hands (presumably a doctor's) is accompanied by the narrator saying, "Operations will be halted midway as believing surgeons are caught up to be forever with the Lord." And I thought it was because patients had really bad health insurance—the kind that only covers the "taking out" part of a liver transplant.

Other Rapturific disasters include "milk deliveries unmade" and "stores remaining closed" (which in consumer America qualifies as a natural disaster). A derelict with darkened patches of skin is betrayed as an unbeliever by his "noisome and grievous sores."

Then the "filmmakers" amp up the terror alert: "Rivers and fountains will be turned into blood. . . . Man will be scorched with great heat. . . . There will be lightning and thunder."

It concludes with the narrator—so stilted he sounds as if he had died halfway through voice-over school—posing the question: "Christians, are you ready for his return?"

Cut to shot of clouds, with the words "Are You Ready?" a final, skywritten spiritual ransom note. A Christian hymn plays wobbily on the soundtrack. Fade to black.

Ed Wood would be proud.

(*The Rapture* is available for downloading at http://www.
archive.org/stream/RAPTURE/RAPTURE.mp4.)

Hal Lindsey's book, *The Late Great Planet Earth,* published in
the 1970s, was the first best-selling book about the Rapture.
Its supporters claim that it has sold 10 million copies and
served as the blueprint for all subsequent Rapturania. A film
version was released in 1979 by American Pictures, an independent company whose other productions have included
Dirt, an epic about teenage dirt bikers.

THE LATE GREAT PLANET EARTH

According to his biographers, Orson Welles professed no religious beliefs, and was looking to subsidize his never-finished
film, *The Other Side of the Wind,* when he took the job as the
sometimes–onscreen narrator of the film version of *The Late
Great Planet Earth.*

The movie—a cinematic ragout of stock footage intercut
with a few dramatic scenes and shots of Welles addressing the
camera—opens with a desert scene. An old hermit in biblical
garb and a Methusaleh-esque beard, looking remarkably like
Michael Palin as the character who introduced every episode of
Monty Python's Flying Circus, is pursued by a group of similarly
berobed young men. They chase him up a cliff and smash him
in the head with a rock, sending him plummeting to his death.

Enter Welles to explain that the old man was a false Hebrew
prophet who was punished for his lack of accuracy. After
discussing the history of the "true" Old Testament prophets,
the film introduces a second old hermit—John of Patmos, the
author or Revelation. The film cursorily enacts the opening
scene in Revelation, when John is visited by the Lord, a young

hunk with white hair, Kabuki makeup, blue eyes, and high cheekbones who resembles a Teutonic Fabio. We hear trumpets.

In his sonorous voice, which producers employed to lend gravitas to everything from B movies to Paul Masson wine, Welles recounts the prophecy that, during the End Times, "There will be no more mountains." Yes, cut to a shot of an exploding mountain.

When Welles quotes Revelation about men who will carry "evil sores," we see a shot of people buried in the sand and trying desperately to crawl out, looking like refugees from a flick called *Beach Blanket Anthrax*. While Welles quotes Revelation about the kingdoms preparing for Armageddon, the film shows a sepia-tinted scene of a stegosaurus that seems to have been filched from a silent film such as *The Lost World* then cuts to a World War II tank attack. (So Armageddon is going to be a war between man and dinosaur?)

At this point, Hal Lindsey appears. A fortyish man in blue jeans and a matching jeans shirt—one of those ugly ones with the shoulder epaulets—modish long hair, and a seventies porn star moustache, he begins to discourse about the imminent End Times.

Scientific experts are trotted out to buttress Lindsey's argument that the end is near; they include one astronomer who predicts that in 1982 Jupiter will exert a magnetic force on the Sun that will cause it to activate all of the Earth's volcanoes. (To be fair, this same scientist also predicted that "in the year 2000, a numskull would become president of the United States.")

Another expert warns that organ transplants, genetic tampering, and other forms of modern technology will create a situation wherein "people will have all their parts replaced and

have an identity crisis." Another avers that our diet has
become so full of toxins that "if the average American man or
woman were submitted to the U.S. Food and Drug Administration for sale as food, he or she wouldn't pass government
standards as being fit for human consumption." Of course this
isn't true—the USDA isn't nearly that discriminating.

Lindsey next discusses Revelation's prediction that the End
Times will be augured by the emergence of "false prophets,"
which he claims is proven by the popularity of occult and
Eastern religions. Thus we see a woman identified as

Babetta
"Witch"

explain why more people are turning to witchcraft, which the
film not-so-subtly damns by cutting to a sinister witchcraft
ceremony lifted from a B horror film.

Student protests (remember: this is the seventies) are cited as
evidence of societal breakdown that will usher in the Antichrist.
He will "appear to be a good man" but will also somehow be "an
American fascist." Cut to Ted Kennedy. I kid you not.

The last five minutes are a montage of apocalyptic images:
mushroom clouds, armies on the plains, and volcanic erup-
tions, all set to martial music. By then, you are just begging
for the End Times to arrive.

Spurred by the success of *The Late Great Planet Earth*, the
Rapture meme snaked into the culture—even to the highest
realms of government. When asked if he believed in the Rapture scenario, born-again George W. Bush has hedged. But he
sure acts as if he can't wait for the end of the world—in Karl
Rove's mind, that's what's called playing to the house.

While his wife hired an in-house astrologer, Ronald Reagan

spoke of the Rapture often, and at one White House state dinner tried to Rapture Mikhail Gorbachev out of his suit.

A filmmaker named Russell S. Doughten, Jr. produced the Thief in the Night series of films in the 1970s and 1980s that dramatizes the Rapture and "the struggles of a small band of believers against an increasingly hostile worldwide Antichrist dictatorship." (*Source:* Wikipedia.) Before that, Doughten's most prominent credit was as producer of the sci-fi film *The Blob*. This is basically the Rapture story, except that God is a bit of interstellar gelatin that enlarges itself by feeding on sinful earthlings, finally is frozen by Steve McQueen, and ends up as Jell-O Magic Mousse (the slogan for which—and you can't tell me this isn't a reference to the Rapture—is "Made in a Wink, Gone in a Flash"). (*Source:* www.kraftfoods.com/jello/)

In 1986, a writer named Frank E. Peretti published a novel titled *This Present Darkness,* which, while neither explicitly mentioning either the Rapture or the Tribulation, does include an Antichrist figure trying to construct a one-world government and centers around spiritual warfare between angels and demons. The concept is lifted from chapter 6 of Paul's letter to the Ephesians, Verse 12: "For our struggle is not against enemies of blood and flesh, but against the rulers, against the authorities, against the cosmic powers of this present darkness, against the spiritual forces of evil in the heavenly places."

(The Satan Antidefamation Society—see chapter 11— called this passage "slanderous and libelous" and sued Paul in heavenly court. They lost the suit, after first requesting a change in venue.)

Peretti's book, which has had eight printings and sold 2 million copies, is set in the "sleepy college town" of Ashton, where an intrepid reporter and a pastor named Hank Busche confront the demonic forces manifesting in a "hideous New Age plot to subjugate the townspeople." (Busche is described as "a novice at prayer," which makes you wonder what the qualifications for pastor are these days.)

Peretti's tale weaves the struggles of Ashton's human characters with (as one Christian book reviewer put it) the "real" struggle behind the scenes: the "spiritual warfare that controls the destinies of men."

> Flailing with swords against forces vastly superior in number, God's angels take their share of blows. A broken wing, a deep gash in the body, pain from countless injuries incurred during moments of lull in the humans' prayer lives. But with every prayer comes a new surge of strength, equipping the angels with the ability to stand against the strongest demons.

Now you know why you haven't been able to sleep at night. World War III is going on right over your head!

> On the other side, lesser demons are terrorized by their superiors, kicked into submission, ridiculed, and abased by every means available to spirit entities. Tiny demons disappear into puffs of smoke, if not at the hands of God's angels, then at the behest of their superiors displeased with their lack of performance. And it seems that, no matter how powerful a demon, there is always one more powerful than he to keep him in place. Jealousy results in a treasonous act by

one demon of high status who is rankled over the impending victory by his hated and abusive superior.

Demons disappearing into puffs of smoke due to poor performance. . . . Who's running this team—George Steinbrenner?

By the novel's end, Pastor Busche gets the hang of that praying thing, and God's team wins (however, they don't cover the spread).

The two people who have done the most to popularize the Rapture in contemporary pop culture are Tim LaHaye and Jerry B. Jenkins. They've sold over 50 million copies of their series of sixteen Left Behind novels and have Mixmastered idiot theology and Clancyesque thriller plots to construct an empire of fear-inducing "entertainment" that includes three films, radio shows, children's books, graphic novels, and video games.

LaHaye, who refers to himself as Doctor, is a Christian minister and political activist who was the idea man for the bestselling Left Behind series. The books, the first of which was published in 1995, are written by Jenkins but are based on LaHaye's interpretation of the prophecies of the Book of Revelation. The success of the first novel in the series led to several sequels, a feature film, *Left Behind: The Movie,* and a series of children's books, Left Behind: The Kids. (See box: Lesser-Known Left Behind Sequels.)

Jenkins, who does the actual writing, claims to be the author of one hundred books.

LEFT BEHIND: THE BOOK—A SYNOPSIS

Just as the Rapture is theology for small children, the Left Behind books are pulp religion, full of one-dimensional characters, insipid dialogue, and clunky, good-versus-evil plots.

In the first volume, also titled *Left Behind,* the protagonist is airline pilot Rayford Steele. Alienated by his wife's recent obsessive evangelicalism, he fantasizes about sexy flight attendant Hattie Durham as he cruises over the Atlantic. Cameron "Buck" Williams, world-famous journalist, is a passenger on the same flight, reflecting on his recent trip to Israel in which he interviewed a Nobel Prize–winning chemist and witnessed an all-out Russian nuclear attack that, halted by a hailstorm and earthquake, miraculously failed to damage a single building or kill a single Jew.

A frenzied Hattie informs Steele that dozens of passengers are missing from the plane. Steele replies, "Well, that's what happens when you fly coach." (Okay, I made that up.)

An elderly woman passenger sits "stunned in the predawn haze, holding her husband's sweater and trousers in her hands." There is no mention of his underwear. Was he wearing any? Do you really want to pursue this?

I thought not.

Cameron realizes that many passengers are missing, and wonders what technology could "remove people from their clothes." Then he remembers: booze.

Buck has the best line, though, when he tells Hattie (who had been hassling him about short-wiring the on-flight phone for use as a modem), "You have to admit, when people disappear, some rules go out the window."

As Steele becomes increasingly aware of the mysterious mass vanishings, he returns home to find that his wife, Irene, has apparently been Raptured. The evidence: her flannel nightgown in the bed where her body had lain. Also her wedding ring. (Heaven is clearly a nudist colony, and bling doesn't get through the metal detectors.) His young son is gone, too. Stricken with remorse, the macho pilot cries himself to sleep.

Buck's friend Dirk Burton, who works in the London financial world, tips him about the sinister meetings of international financiers who are backing an obscure Romanian politician, Nicolae Carpathia, and have decided to create a single global currency. (*Note:* It is not Casino Bucks.)

Steele, unable to get through to his daughter Chloe at Stanford, regrets not taking his wife's Christian badgering seriously. He fears that he'll suffer eternally in hell for his arrogant pride, and wonders if there are any "options" left. Like what—another Rapture? Does he think there's going to be a shuttle taking people from Chicago to Heaven?

Steele tries reading the Book of Revelation but, like everybody else, finds it senseless.

The pilot lands Buck in Easton, Pennsylvania, which, he tells Buck, is the "old stompin' grounds of Larry Holmes. . . . If he was still around, whoever was takin' people might've got a knock on the noggin from ol' Larry."

Yeah. Larry Holmes versus God (aka the Great White Hope).

Steele and Chloe visit Bruce, the assistant pastor of their church, who admits to having been a spiritual phony and justifiably Left Behind. Bruce gives them a copy of the Raptured pastor's "Left Behind" tape, and implores them to accept Christ.

Steele—unlike his skeptical daughter—is convinced. "It had become an ugly world overnight. . . . People checked the graves of loved ones to see if their corpses had disappeared." (This brings up another question: the souls of dead Christians are supposed to be Raptured along with those of the living. What if the dead Christian donated his kidney to a heathen

Left Behind? Would the kidney be Raptured while the rest of the heathen's body was Left Behind? Just asking . . .)

Bruce the assistant pastor asks Steele to have lunch. You see, he needs someone to talk to. (Now we know why the guy wasn't Raptured. If your pastor is needier than you are, your church is in bad shape.)

Steele watches the tape. The pastor explains that the Rapture is God's "final effort to get the attention of every person who has ignored or rejected him." Where I come from, we call that acting out.

The pastor warns Steele of the Antichrist, a "world leader who will step forward with signs and wonders that will be so impressive many will believe he is of God," and of the seven-year Tribulation. Then, to Steele's dismay, the tape cuts to a commercial for Sizzler.

Robbers, emboldened by the breakdown in civil authority occasioned by the Rapture, break into Steele's home and take all his valuables. Steele says, "It's as if the inner city has moved to the suburbs. We're no safer here anymore." Here LaHaye and Jenkins betray the prejudices of their background and that of their readers: white Christian suburbanites. (Think: Colorado Springs.) *Left Behind* is a lily-white book; there isn't one African-American, Latino, or Asian character save a black female bureau chief in Buck's company— a minor figure—who is beamed up on Rapture day (in the back of the heavenly bus).

I'm going to cut out a lot of stuff here. Suffice it to say that the authors' loopy plot brings together Steele, Chloe, Buck, and Hattie, who becomes the mistress of the Antichrist, quits her career, and devotes herself full time to evildoing.

Carpathia reveals dastardliness worthy of the Antichrist in the book's climactic scene; in full view of international dignitaries, he shoots two financiers and hypnotizes the witnesses into believing it was a suicide. Not even David Blaine would try to pull that off.

In the end, all the main characters become self-lacerating converts to Christianity, mentally flogging themselves for not having sooner recognized God's omnipotence, yadda, yadda. . . .

LESSER-KNOWN *LEFT BEHIND* SEQUELS

- *Left Behind: The Car Keys*

- *Left Behind: The Cat*

- *Left Even More Behind*

- *Left Behind: Not Again?*

- *Left Behind: My Favorite Pair of Fuck-Me Pumps*

- *Left Behind: Incriminating Shots of Me with a Congressional Page*

- *Left Behind: Hillary Clinton*

- *Left Behind: The Fifty Bucks I Owe You*

- *Ernest: Left Behind*

LEFT BEHIND: THE MOVIE
Left Behind: The Movie was made by Cloud Ten Pictures, which claims to be the first full-fledged Christian film studio.

Cloud Ten has made films such as *Revelation* starring Gary Busey, the former drug addict (with twelve restraining orders for—in his words—"being too real") turned born-again Christian whose role as an evil gun-running Jew in a Turkish film got him accused of medieval anti-Semitic blood libel.

Before its theatrical release, the producers hawked the film to the Christian community, who ate it up to the tune of 2.8 million videos sold.

Some highlights:

- The actual Rapture scene, in which Chloe, who has come upon a scene of highway-crash carnage, opens the door to a semitruck cab and finds only a pair of overalls on the seat. Gone to trucker Heaven—a country song waiting to happen.
- Chloe returns home and finds Buck—who she has never met before and who has taken temporary refuge with Steele—sleeping on the sofa. "Buck Williams, what are you doing on my couch?" Yes, it's not everyday you that find that a famous anchorperson has crashed in your home. "Wolf Blitzer, what are you doing in my bed?"
- A private plane pilot and Buck discuss explanations for the missing people. The pilot says, "The real question is if people have gone for good, or if they'll be sent back."

Now, it never occurred to me that some of the Raptured would be returned to Earth, that God could act like a dissatisfied customer who takes home his purchase only to find it damaged. (And let's face it: *He* wouldn't need a receipt.) So I started thinking about what it would take to be Raptured, then returned, and came up with the following list:

- Caught bringing liquids and/or gels onto the flight
- Found with an ACLU membership card in your wallet
- Overheard admitting to another Raptured person that you were "strangely moved" by Andres Serrano's "Piss Christ"
- Disrupting the flight in an argument over a window seat.
- Telling the Lord that the Rapture can't hold a candle to Space Mountain
- At the time of the Rapture, you just happened to have a butt plug in the shape of Jesus inserted in your rectum. (*Note:* A company named Divine Intervention actually makes such an item.)
- Offhandedly quipping to a friend that the Rapture would've been even better on acid

Anyway, the rest of the film is even worse with dialogue such as "World peace: it's been a dream ever since Cain looked sideways at Abel."

But don't take my word for it. Here's what the critics had to say about *Left Behind: the Movie*:

- For all its intimations of fire and brimstone, the film isn't remotely frightening, and the high-school-level acting doesn't help.
  —Stephen Holden, *New York Times*

- It may have seemed plausible on paper, but *Left Behind* . . . just looks ludicrous on screen.
  —John Monaghan, *Detroit Free Press*

- Whatever the central message, the movie's still a blundering cringefest, thanks to unintentionally laughable dialogue, hackneyed writing and uninspired direction.
  —Desson Thomson, *Washington Post*

- So awful that even true believers will have difficulty staying awake.
  —Glenn Whipp, *Los Angeles Daily News*

- These folks get eternity in Heaven, while I'm stuck here watching [*Left Behind*]. I'm calling my rabbi.
  —Scott Weinberg, *DVD Talk*

- Nearly unendurable.
  —Tom Keough, Film.com

- After watching *Left Behind,* all I can say is: Now I know I made the right decision.
  —Satan

Of course, all of these critics will be Left Behind. Their punishment: for the rest of eternity they will have to pay for screenings.

The *Left Behind* DVD's "Special Features" are no better than the film. They include the "Hollywood premiere" of *Left Behind,* in which an *Entertainment Tonight*–like woman reporter interviews celebrities such as Tom Selleck and Corbin Bernsen while

> ## THE MAKING OF THE RAPTURE
>
> After the Rapture, will God release a *Making of the Rapture* DVD showing you exactly how he pulled it off—the special effects and so forth—and interviews with some of the Raptured people?
>
> "I'm thrilled. When my agent got the call, I, like, freaked! I mean, I'm His biggest fan."
>
> "Even better than working with Woody."
>
> "Just an amazing experience. I'd work with him again—anytime—without even seeing a script."

demonic disco music pulsates in the background. And there's the obligatory "Making Of" documentary, in which the actors blather on about how thrilled they were to participate, and one of the producers actually says, "The success of this movie depends on a lot of people going to see it."

When the film was released in 2000, there was a *Left Behind* title song, music video, and concert tour to accompany it. The same producers subsequently filmed two other volumes in the Left Behind series. It's clear that LeHay and Jenkins believe that the Rapture not only is a cataclysmic historical event but also a killer brand, and it's not hard to anticipate their seizing other merchandising opportunities, such as:

- A Rapture T-shirt with special personalized slogans such as *I Got Raptured and All* (name of your ex-husband here) *Got Was a Lousy T-Shirt, the Bastard.*
- A Rapture coffee mug that reads, *It's Been a Wild Ride.*

THE ADULT FILM INDUSTRY TAKES ON THE RAPTURE

As is the norm in our decadent society, the adult film industry has tried to capitalize on the Rapture phenomenon with a series of porn flicks that will have only the slimmest relation to the end of days:

- *Left in Her Behind.* Lexis DeVille plays a lapsed Christian who is seduced by a Satanic cult led by Hard Johnny Rodd. To punish them, God, played by Ron Jeremy, turns Lexis, Rodd, and the entire cult into Jersey landfill. But not before girl-boy, girl-girl, boy-boy, boy-girl-zucchini, girl-Fleet enema, and Jell-O Magic Mousse orgy scenes. Warning: must be eighteen to view. At the end of the film, the Lord will make your DVD player explode.

- *Ass-ageddon.* After the battle between God and Satan, Rexella Stephens is the last nympho left on Earth. Rod LaCock, Brad Tumescent, and Woody Woodman lead a band of survivalists into Rexella's anal cavity, until the Lord, while holding his nose, smites them all dead.

- *God Likes to Watch.* Brianna Blow and Suzi Sukiyaki realize that God's omniscience means he is watching them have sex, so they go out of their way to taunt him. (e.g., "Looky here, God baby—I'm using a strap-on!"). God responds by sending them to the circle of Hell where sinners spend eternity face-first in lube.

- *Gunfight at the Beefcake Ranch.* Rex Blueballs and Adam Adonis cornhole their way through the Tribulation as cowboys trying to protect their ranch from flying dragons.

- A Secret Book of Revelation Decoder Ring. For the kids.
- A special Rapture-ready clothing line with Velcro snaps to make it easy for you to be Raptured out of them.

LEFT BEHIND: THE VIDEO GAME

Message to New Yorkers: you thought having to contend with noise, crime, polluted air, apartments so small they're ruled strictly by the laws of quantum physics, and besotted bridge-and-tunnelers on their way to Crobar urinating on your sidewalks was bad enough. But being Left Behind will make you yearn for the days when your biggest problem was trying to decipher MTA subway announcements.

That's if you believe the makers of *Left Behind: Eternal Forces,* a video game based on LaHaye and Jenkins's oeuvre and created by two Jews who have converted to—or been "completed by," as they put it—Christianity.

Eternal Forces is set in contemporary New York City. The citizens Left Behind after all of the true Christians have been Raptured are to be converted or killed by a roving Christian militia composed not only of tanks, snipers, and infantrymen, but also evangelical ministers. These religious leaders battle the "Global Community," comprised of a United Nations peacekeeping force headed by the Antichrist, along with "rock stars" and "cult leaders."

Yup, it's God's army against Van Halen.

And we learn that the Antichrist, Carpathia, is actually the bioengineered son of two gay men—the Bionic Queer. Bet you didn't know that all this time the gay community was secretly bent on turning planet Earth into planet Fabulous.

On their Web site, the creators of *Eternal Forces* promise players that they can:

- "Conduct physical & spiritual warfare . . . recover ancient scriptures and witness spectacular . . . demonic activity." Especially if your platoon happens to get lost in Chelsea during Cabaret Week.
- "Command your forces through intense battles across a breathtaking, authentic depiction of New York City." However, make sure not to order your troops into a suicidal position, such as defending the Jimmy Choo counter during a sale at Bergdorf's.
- "Control more than thirty unit types—from Prayer Warrior and Hellraiser to Spies, Special Forces and Battle Tanks!" Prayer Warrior? What does he do, shoot Bibles out of a bazooka? (Tip to heathens: The only thing that can repel a machine-gunned Bible is a copy of *The Communist Manifesto* placed over your heart.)

If *Eternal Forces* is your idea of a can't-miss video game, you might enjoy other games based on biblical themes, such as *Who Raided Jesus' Tomb?* and *Leviticus: The Game* (in which you are an ancient Israelite who has to try to figure out which laws apply to the eating of clean and unclean animals).

THE CHRISTIAN FILM INDUSTRY

If you don't count *The Passion of the Christ, Left Behind* is the most successful product in the history of the Christian film industry, which began in the 1940s. For many years, Christian films were hindered by the lack of a distribution network (there were no Christian movie theaters). Most of them were 16 mm affairs such as *The Rapture,* shown in churches and available through Christian libraries.

A Thief in the Night and its successors—in fact, most of the Christian feature films—are adaptations of events in Revelation. Why depend so heavily on one biblical book? Well, who in their right mind would want to sit through a film called *The Passion of Deuteronomy?* Or how about *Numbers: The Movie?* (with Moses taking the roll call of Israelites fit for military service. . . .)

In the 1980s, John Schmidt produced a popular youth film called *Super Christian* whose protagonist is a regular guy during the week and a Christian on weekends. (Hollywood producer: "Make him a Satanist during the week, and we've got a deal.") Schmidt went on to release *Kevin, The Greatest Story Never Told,* and *Super Christian 2.*

To avoid sitting through these movies, Jesus would even renounce his Father.

By 2006, the box-office potential of Christian movies was starting to attract major studios. New Line Cinema released *Nativity Story,* and Fox Films announced it was creating FoxFaith, a division devoted to Christian films. Born-again producer David Kirkpatrick said that he intended to roll out religious films in what he considered a battle for the hearts and minds of teenagers. He added that the most obvious method would be "Christian horror films,"* and that he—along with the

Weinstein Company—was negotiating to adapt for the screen one of the Dudleytown series of Christian horror novels, named for a now-abandoned town in Connecticut that was said to be cursed.

The oldest trick in the organized religion playbook: if you can't persuade 'em, scare 'em to death. Let's speculate on some of the Christian horror flicks you can expect to see at your nearest camp meeting:

- *The Jesus Chainsaw Massacre* (The humble carpenter goes berserk after some bullies break his lathe.)

- *I Know How Much You Put in the Collection Basket Last Sunday*

- *The Dirty Dozen II* (The Apostles vow vengeance on the Jews and Romans and, while we don't want to give away the plot, it involves a zombie army.)

- *Saint Augustine Meets Dracula*

- *The Liberal from 20,000 Fathoms* (A giant sea creature that looks just like Barney Frank threatens to destroy a complacent Christian community.)

Don't think that Satan is going to take this cinematic offensive lying down. Odds are the Evil One will open up his own filmmaking center. . . . Oh, wait, he already has. It's called Hollywood.

* *New York Times*, December 11, 2006.

THE TRIBULATION MOVIE–*SIX: THE MARK UNLEASHED*

Six: The Mark Unleashed, released in 2004 by a company called Christian Cinema, is part of a rapidly growing cinematic subgenre: the End Times thriller. Other titles include the Apocalypse series, *The Omega Code, The Evangelism Trilogy, Years of the Beast, Final Exit,* and other films so awful that they aren't even good enough to show during the Rapture. (See box in chapter 9: Rapture In-Flight Movies.)

Six only differs from your typical Bruce Willis macho-fest in that it delivers a typical Christian message—accept Jesus or burn—and it was made for about as much money as Jerry Bruckheimer tips the valet at Spago. Also, its title is ungrammatical. You can't unleash (or leash, for that matter) a mark. A beast, yes . . .

In Hollywood-pitch terms, *Six* is *Gattica* meets *The Passion of the Christ* meets *Die Hard*. It opens with a newsreel shot of Hitler and stars Billy Baldwin, so right from the start you know to fasten your seat belts, it's going to be one campy ride.

Six is set in the dystopian future. Although the film doesn't allude to it explicitly, Rapturologists will immediately recognize the time period as that of the Tribulation—just as they will infer that *Six* is the Mark of the Beast, a computer chip implanted by the Antichrist (here called the Leader) and his minions in most of Earth's population.

The film opens with a gorgeous Asian woman (and as it turns out, ex-*Playboy* video star) delineating the attributes of the "holy implant" on a telescreen to an audience of newly implanted, zombified subjects. "Such primitive emotions and ideas as jealousy, rage, and monogamy have been eliminated," she says. "Your new implant has made you part of a collective whole known as the community . . . where you are truly free to move among partners, male and female, as you choose. Your pleasure will be your guide."

Already, we get the Christian message: Religion and suffering—good. Free love and brotherhood—bad.

The rest of the film can be synopsized thusly: Brody and Jerry, two young renegade dudes, are apprehended by the Leader's Gestapo and are forced to choose between having the chip implanted and death by guillotine. They are taken to witness a beheading of refuseniks. Afterward in their cell, Jerry, a computer nerd, says to Brody, a surfer type, "You seem depressed." "I'm a little depressed," replies wiseass Brody. "Something about watching people get their heads cut off gets me down." Then they discuss how long disembodied heads can stay alive.

Call it *Bill and Ted's Most Excellent Tribulation.*

Meanwhile, the feds arrest Dallas, an ex-LAPD cop and black marketer who has refused to accept the Mark of the Beast and whose ex-wife, Jessica, has gone over to the dark side. (Her impassive expression throughout must mean that her mark came with extra Botox.) A shaven-headed Dr. Evil type with raccoonish circles under his eyes and a vampiric pallor tortures Dallas by putting him in an Iron Maiden, positioning him like Christ on the cross, and "simulating" various torments, such as "having broken glass shoved into every orifice in your body." Move over, Mel Gibson; there's a new sadist in town.

Dallas agrees to go undercover in the Christian community and assassinate Elijah Cohen, a prophet (Elijah the prophet, get it?) who is "preaching the Christian message."

Heavy-lidded Billy Baldwin (the right-wing Baldwin) makes his first appearance in the film as Luke, a Christian zealot in the adjoining cell to Brody and Jerry's. In the mess hall, he and Brody argue about evolution, and surfer dude Brody suddenly raises the cosmological argument against God's existence. It's as if Spicoli started channeling Teilhard de Chardin.

A bit later, Luke converts Jerry to Christianity. When Jerry tells Brody about his newfound faith, Brody petulantly demands that he "take it back." (*Note:* During the Spanish Inquisition, Torquemada demanded the same thing of the heretics.)

Following is a car chase, one of several, that involves Dallas, Brody, and Jerry escaping to Prodigal City, a Christian kibbutz. On the way, they stop at an Underground Railroad safe house for believers. There, Brody meets a former hooker-turned-hypnotized Christian named Rahab (an anagram of "Ahab in rehab"?), who comes on to him. But when he responds, she backs off: "I'm faithful to Jesus now, but if you stick around we could get married."

Women . . .

Dallas, Jerry, and Brody escape just as the Gestapo agents arrive and murder Rahab. (You see, in the future, it is illegal to have a ridiculous name.) Dallas learns from Jerry that the Leader, via a global satellite network, is constantly sending signals to the implants that "directly affect the brain, alter personality, and remove or add inhibitions." You mean, just like television?

Dallas decides to try to disable the satellites and forces Jessica to sneak them into the Leader's computer nerve center. Jerry, trying to hack into the system, alerts security, and the trio appears to be trapped by Zach, a blind minister of the Leader, and his goons. However, Elijah appears out of nowhere and freezes the bad guys.

Loony *ex machina.*

Dallas, Jerry, and Brody head to Prodigal City. Jerry stays. Dallas and Brody decide to leave, and are immediately apprehended.

The film's final scene has Dallas back in the Iron Maiden, his face ecstatic with pain as he accepts the Lord into his heart. In the born-again Christian world, this is what passes for a happy ending.

OTHER GLOBAL CONSPIRACIES
THE CHRISTIAN RIGHT BELIEVES

You might say that believers in the Rapture view it as a biblical conspiracy invented by God and involving Satan, various other otherworldly creatures, and all of humanity.

Here are some other conspiracy theories that the Christian right entertains:

- A race of reptilian creatures called the Babylonian Brotherhood secretly controls the world. Its members include Howard Dean, the UN, the IRS, and that box turtle your son keeps in his bedroom.

- The Elders of Zion, a Jewish group that secretly controls the world and meets clandestinely in a retirement home in Boca Raton. You'll stop laughing when you wake up one day to find that all meals are early-bird specials.

- Area 52, a remote part of Nevada where aliens who crash-landed on Earth in 1947 play golf with American generals.

- The secret government warehouses in which are stored the Ark of the Covenant, the Holy Grail, and all of humanity's lost socks.

- Satanic cults are kidnapping our children and brainwashing them to appear on reality TV shows.

RAPTURE BUMPER STICKERS

Rapture devotees aren't shy about advertising their lunacy. If they can't proselytize personally, they'll thrust their beliefs out their tailpipe so you can feel inferior/scared/guilt-ridden while choking on their exhaust fumes. One hugely popular bumper sticker reads, *In case of Rapture, this car will be unmanned.* Hey, thanks for the warning.

Here are some others:

- IN CASE OF RAPTURE, CALL AAA.

- JESUS IS COMING AGAIN—THIS TIME IT'S PERSONAL!

- DON'T GET LEFT BEHIND—GO TO CLEM'S AUTO BODY.

- CHRISTIANS DO IT . . . STRICTLY FOR PROCREATION.

- REPENT, THE END (OF PAPA EARL'S $1.99 CAJUN CHICKEN SPECIAL) IS NEAR.

Not everyone is crazy about the Rapture or tolerant of its devotees. Some Americans are enraged at the sheer regressive stupidity of it. People like Harvey Saperstein . . .

BORN-AGAIN CHRISTIANS SHOULD BE MADE TO LIVE LIKE THEY DID IN CHRIST'S TIME

By Harvey Saperstein, the atheist insult comic

These *fakakta* born-again people want to take the Bible literally and impose laws taken from the Old Testament on twenty-first-century America, right? Then you know what I say? You want to take the Bible literally, then you gotta go all the way! I would force these schmucks to adopt the following biblical ways:

- They should have names only found in the Bible, like Zebediah or Beelzebub. Oh, yeah, those are real chick magnets! Or how about Bathsheba. Or Hagar. Sounds like you should be wearing pelts and carrying a spear. Gad. Yes, that's an actual biblical name. "Hi, I'm Gad."—"Gad to know you." Methuselah. Ahab. Imagine going through life with a name like Ahab. "Hi, I'm Ahab." "And I'm Moby Dick." "Aye-aye, Captain." Sick.

- They should wear biblical garb made only of materials known to the inhabitants of Judea two thousand years ago. "Hey, Job, I know it's Casual Friday, but don't you think that loincloth is taking things a bit too far?"

- No central heating, electricity, or indoor plumbing. And no bitching about it.

- They must drive to work in an oxcart; it should be their only means of transportation. That, or a Fred Flintstone car they propel with their feet.

- They must speak in an ancient tongue such as Aramaic.

- All PowerPoint presentations they make at the office have to be done on stone tablets.

- When they get fired, they must not preach in the parking lot: "Castelli Brothers Cadillac Dealership Unfair to First-Century Christians."

- They must be made to live on manna. If no manna is available, then Wonder Bread.

- Instead of the Internet, they get the Wise Men.

- No rights for women. And forget animals!

- They must express primitive incredulity at modern conveniences, that is, "An oxcart that can fly! And without oxen! That ought to teach 'em.

CHAPTER FIVE

Signs That the Rapture Is Near, or It's Not Global Warming, Stupid

SIGNS THAT THE RAPTURE IS NEAR

The Gospel of Matthew records Jesus prophesizing to his disciples about his messianic return to Earth and listing the many auguries of His second coming. However, we now know that this Gospel, like many early Christian teachings, was edited after Jesus' time. Now, for the first time, is the complete list of the phenomena signaling the End Times:

- Wars and rumors of wars
- Nation will rise against nation
- East Coast rapper will rise against West Coast rapper
- Famines
- Obesity epidemic
- Floods
- Overturned tractor trailers

- *So You Think You Can Dance?*
- Earthquakes
- The Kansas City Royals will win the World Series.
- Animals will begin to speak, and they will take over talk radio.
- Many false prophets will arise and deceive many. They will all wear false beards.
- Due to excessive lawlessness, the love of many will grow cold. However, the Internet porn will be more popular than ever.
- Cloning, especially of sheep
- The Four Horsemen of the Apocalypse will appear, and one of them will win the Kentucky Derby and pay 100–1.
- George W. Bush will win the Nobel Peace Prize.

Rapturologists have long obsessed over the signs of the Antichrist's emergence. The following is a list of his identifying traits:

- He will arise from somewhere in eastern Europe. Specifically, Transylvania.
- The entire world will worship him, except for some parts of the American South, where he will not be considered right wing enough.
- He will have his own cologne, called 666.
- During an appearance on the *Charlie Rose Show*, he will make Charlie bark like a dog.
- He will become head of a major corporation and institute a new employee policy: Take Your Mistress to Work Day.

- He will head a one-world government, and his vice president will be Al Gore. (Later, Gore will boast, "I invented one-world government.")
- He will unveil a government program that will subsidize evil. He will name it the Department of Homeland Security.
- He will wear Prada. And look smashing.

Perhaps the most obvious omen of the Rapture's imminence will be the phenomenon reported in this news story, which hit the wires just as this book went to press:

JUDGE RULES PLEDGE OF ALLEGIANCE MUST MENTION SATAN

WASHINGTON—Citing the principle of equal time, a federal court judge ruled today that the Pledge of Allegiance must include a reference to Satan. Conservatives reacted with shock and outrage to the ruling by Second Court of Appeals Judge Wendy Williams. The judge made the ruling in response to a lawsuit filed by Hell's Lobbyists, a Devil-worshipping political action group, who contended that the words "under God" added to the pledge after the fact were prejudicial to devotees of Satan.

Right-wing groups such as the Pro-Life Abortionist Killers said they would appeal the ruling to the Supreme Court "and, if necessary, the court above them." Donald Wildmon, executive director of the American Family Foundation, called the ruling "the worst judicial decision since they gave blacks the vote," and said that "once you invite Satan into the Pledge, who's next—Ed Asner?"

Meanwhile, various versions of the "Dark Pledge," as it immediately became known, have begun to circulate among Washington officials. The one most likely to become standard in America's schools reads, "I pledge allegiance to the Flag of the United States of America and to the Republic for which it stands, one nation, under God, indivisible, with liberty and justice for all—Hail Satan!"

THE RAPTURE INDEX

For centuries, End Timers had tried to determine the exact date of the Rapture. But until recently, they were forced to rely on such unscientific methods as entrail reading, palmistry, the prophecies of Nostradamus, and whatever they could decipher from reading the Bible. No wonder they've gotten the date wrong for two thousand years.

Fortunately, we in the twenty-first century have devised a much more accurate method for pinpointing the exact date for the end of the world.

It's called the Rapture Index, a kind of Dow Jones Average for the End Times set. It tracks not stocks, but signs of the Apocalypse: earthquakes, floods, plagues, crime, false prophets, unemployment (especially among false prophets), instability, and civil unrest—anything that according to Revelation would ease the way for the Antichrist. (Financial tip: Do *not* let your mutual fund manager place your retirement savings in the Rapture Index. The Apocalypse is not a growth industry.)

The Rapture Index is an invention of Todd Strandberg, a night supervisor at the spare-parts store at Offutt Air Force base in Nebraska, who was frustrated at the lack of standardization of End Times prognostication. "You had the white-haired guy with the sign wigging out in front of Costco saying the End was near, and the other white-haired guy with the sign wigging out in front of Wal-mart saying the End was nearer. Talk about confusing," said Strandberg. (Full disclosure: Strandberg is a real person. The quote is fictional, although not false.)

Strandberg, who publishes the constantly updated Index on his site, Raptureready.com, uses dozens of factors to arrive at his Index number. Some of them include:

- Satanism (He determines the nationwide rate of Satanic activity by polling Americans at random and asking them, "How many goats have you sacrificed to the Evil One this week?")
- Unemployment, inflation, interest rates, and the reappearance of Alan Greenspan
- Price of oil, as measured in shekels
- Standings of the English Premier Football League
- Rate of gay massages for Christian ministers
- Supernatural activity, such as untainted elections
- Number of new specials at the One Hung Lo Chinese restaurant
- Instances of "Beast Government," such as an orangutan who got elected sheriff in Arizona and the mutant half rat, half Republicans running Congress
- Wild weather (blizzards, hurricanes, plagues, flying nuns)

Judging from a brief perusal of RaptureReady, a fair number of evangelicals are stricken with ennui and looking for God to do what they're too timid to try themselves. Listen to the chorus of demoralized voices on one thread. (*Note:* Text unaltered from site.)

- [A recent sermon suggesting the Rapture was not imminent] . . . just really discouraged me. And maybe I am crazy, but I don't want to live here until I am old. I want to see Jesus. . . . ☹ I am tired of watching and waiting. Just weary I guess.

- I sometimes get tired of waiting too.
- Me too!!! I want it to be today!!!
- It's just a longing you know. . . . I can't explain it
  . . . a groaning to see my Lord." [Funny, I got
  that same feeling after eating at Popeyes'.]
- If you see Jesus via Rapture or the 'old fashion
  way' called death, what difference does it make?
  You still get to see Him. Right? "☺ [That's tech-
  nically correct, Mr. Smiley Face, but I'll take my
  chances with the Grim Reaper. At least he'll let
  me keep my clothes on.]
- Lets not forget a lot of church's now a day try to
  make the Bible more palettable to more people, a
  lot of blind and lost people don't like to hear
  things like the rapture and the coming of Christ
  or the truth for that matter. So a lot of preachers
  candy coat the scriptures so it is more appealing
  to the masses. A sign of the End Times. [Another
  sign of the End Times—candy-coating the scriptures. You know: Jonah plays with the dolphins.
  God teases Job. Sodom and Gomorrah just have
  to pay fines. That sort of thing.]

Only one respondent seems to have thought through this
Rapture thing: "I think the best thing to do is live your life as
if there was no rapture. Act as though you have never heard
the word. People that bury their head in the sand and only
think of the rapture, like I did at one time, will end up having
issues with faith and many other biblical things."

Amen.

CHAPTER SIX

Televangelists and Other Public Figures Who Believe They Will Be Raptured, but Who Most Definitely Won't Be

The powerful Christian-right wing nuts—Jerry Falwell, Pat Robertson, James Dobson and the like—are convinced that when the Rapture comes, God's going to send His stretch limo to pick them up. But a survey of their multifarious crimes and misdemeanors reveals they're more likely to be Left Behind to preach to the riffraff.

JERRY FALWELL

In a 2006 interview on *Paula Zahn Now*, Falwell, a founder of the Moral Majority. claimed, "I believe in the premillenial, pretribulational coming of Christ for all of his church."

However, when Jesus makes his Second Coming, Falwell's

going to have some 'splainin' to do. In the 1990s, the Securities & Exchange Commission charged Falwell with fraud and deceit in the issuance of $6.5 million in unsecured church bonds issued by Falwell's organizations. (I'm not a biblical scholar, but I can't remember Jesus preaching, "Thou shall sell IOUs to make some quick up-front cash.")

During Clinton's presidency, Falwell produced a documentary accusing him of engaging in cocaine smuggling and implicated him in the deaths of Vincent Foster and paid off state troopers to make defamatory accusations against Clinton—all of which were proven to be false and driven by Falwell's desire to destroy Clinton's political career.

What else? Falwell blamed the 9/11 attacks on feminists, gays, and the ACLU. (Not only were nebbishy Jewish lawyers piloting those planes, but they were working pro bono.)

In 1999, an article in Falwell's *National Liberty Journal* suggested that Tinky Winky, a *Telletubbies* character, could be a hidden gay symbol, because the character was purple (a color symbolic of homosexuality, according to the Rev), had an inverted triangle on his head, and carried a handbag. (He also charged Dora the Explorer with being a bull dyke.)

Falwell demonstrated his cynical motives when he told Mel White, the gay ghostwriter of his autobiography, "Thank God for these gay demonstrators. If I didn't have them, I'd have to invent them. They give me all the publicity I need." (*Source:* "Religion, Politics a Potent Mix for Jerry Falwell," www.npr.org, June 30, 2006.)

He also has claimed that God is a Republican, Jesus is the "first American," and that the public school system should be destroyed and replaced by Christian education.

Odds of being Raptured: 600–1.

Only chance: bribe the guy holding the Rapture switch.

Act of desperation: accuse Jesus of being gay. (He never married, hung out exclusively with twelve men, preached peace and brotherhood.)

JIM BAKKER

Bakker was a proponent of "prosperity theology" and author of *Prosperity and the Coming Apocalypse* (or How to Profit from the End of the World), founder of the PTL televangelism network and husband of Tammy Faye Bakker. In 1987, after receiving millions in salary and bonuses from PTL, Bakker was forced to resign following threats that someone would reveal he'd paid $265,000 to former secretary Jessica Hahn to keep quiet about sexual services she provided him. Hahn was only one of many B-girls who Bakker was sanctifying with his penis.

A later investigation into financial irregularities at PTL and its Heritage USA Christian-oriented theme park led to Bakker being indicted on federal charges of fraud, tax evasion, and racketeering that included his appropriation of church funds to buy, among other luxury items, condos and a Rolls Royce and to have their clothing flown first class across the country. He was convicted and sentenced to forty-five years. (The sentence was later reduced to eighteen years, of which he served five before being released to make room for other Christian ministers.)

Despite his long-lasting public humiliation, Bakker unashamedly exploited his crimes by publishing a book, titled *I Was Wrong*, in which he finally admitted he hadn't read the

Bible "all the way through." (I mean, he tried, but using his penis as a divining rod was so much more fun. So he limited himself to the parts that seemed to justify his being made a multimillionaire by his followers' slavish donations.) Having expressed ersatz repentance, Bakker and his new wife returned to the airwaves in 2003 with *The New Jim Bakker Show.* When it comes to resurrections, Jesus had nothing on this guy.

Odds of being Raptured: 1000–1

Only chance: if God feels that he's already suffered enough by being married to Tammy Faye, a golem made out of spare bits found in a plastic surgeon's biohazard bin.

Act of desperation: reveals that Tammy Faye was a drag queen named Norman.

PAT ROBERTSON

Founder of the Christian Broadcasting Network and The Christian Coalition—one of the most influential lobbying groups in the country—creator/host of *The 700 Club* and one-time Republican presidential candidate, Robertson remains not only one of America's most powerful evangelists, but the only one to market his own weight-loss shake (with his partner, GNC).

Here's some evidence God may use in determining Robertson's Rapture-worthiness:

- Tries entering into a joint agreement with the Bank of Scotland to provide financial services to U.S. consumers, but the bank cancels the venture after Robertson comments that Scotland was "a dark land overrun by homosexuals." (I mean, the kilts are a dead giveaway.)

- Invests $8 million in a Liberian gold mine and publicly advocates for President Charles Taylor, who the UN had indicted for war crimes
- Uses his tax-exempt, nonprofit organization, Operation Blessing, as a front for his own financial gain, and when he's caught, gets Republican power brokers to exculpate him
- Robertson makes emotional pleas on *The 700 Club* for cash donations to Operation Blessing to support airlifts of refugees from Rwanda to Zaire. Then a reporter discovers that Operation Blessing's planes were transporting diamond-mining equipment for the African Development Corporation, a venture Robertson had established in cooperation with Zaire's murderous dictator, Mobuto Sese Seko. Robertson is exonerated by the Virginia attorney general, to whom he had made a mega–campaign contribution.
- Claims that the Episcopalians are harboring the Antichrist. (The tip-off was the title of Sunday's sermon: "Worship the Goat!")
- Calls for the public assassination of Hugo Chavez.
- Declares that feminism encourages people to kill their children, practice witchcraft, become lesbians, and destroy capitalism. Also, that acceptance of homosexuality could result in hurricanes, earthquakes, tornadoes, terrorist bombings, and possibly a meteor. That's right, Pat, don't go out

on a limb. (Memo to Rosie O'Donnell: order that interstellar collision insurance.)

- Claims at age seventy-eight to have leg-pressed two thousand pounds, over six hundred pounds more than the world's record.

A telecommunications billionaire, Pat thinks he's doing the Lord's work. After all, didn't Jesus say, "Be fruitful and diversify"?

Odds of being Raptured: less than zero. In any sane, moral society, he'd be in a special cage reserved for the lowest of the low—a cage he'd share with health insurance execs, Big Pharma, and Thomas Friedman. And the U.S. government, all the other corporate CEOs, the mainstream media, Vladimir Putin, all the other governments and . . . ach, you might as well place the entire Earth in a cage, except for me, my editor, Carl Bromley, my representatives, Imprint Agency, Inc., and . . . if you don't want to end up in the cage, I'd buy this book.

Only chance: if God grades the Last Judgment on a humongous curve.

Act of desperation: tries to assassinate Fidel Castro by leg-pressing him to death.

(*Source:* Wikipedia.)

JAMES DOBSON

In 2005, Dobson, founder of a conservative Christian group called Focus on the Family and a radio program of the same name that appears on six hundred stations, told members of Congress that SpongeBob had been included in a pro-homosexual video which was to be mailed to thousands of elementary schools to push on students a tolerance pledge that included an acceptance of what Dobson called "sexual identity." Dobson added that most of the popular kids' TV characters conspired in the plot, including Barney and Jimmy Neutron.

Questions: Why do these fundamentalist ministers watch so much Saturday-morning TV? Shouldn't they be talking to God? And why do they see so much deviance and perversion behind every innocent cartoon? Of what variety of Saturday-morning cartoons would they approve? (See box: Christian Right Saturday Morning Cartoon Shows.)

And why does he want to damn cartoon characters? It's like he wants God to send SpongeBob to cartoon hell, where he'll spend the rest of eternity with Betty Boop and Fritz the Cat.

Dobson has been called the most influential evangelical in America, and his bête noire is gay people: he spent more than a half-million dollars to promote a constitutional amendment to ban same-sex marriage in its home state of Colorado.

Odds of being Raptured: 800–1.

Only chance: he gets mistakenly swept up in a Rapture dragnet.

Act of desperation: attempts to ban comic strip "Blondie" because eponymous character "gives too much grief to Dagwood."

CHRISTIAN RIGHT SATURDAY MORNING CARTOON SHOWS

- *Casper, the Holy Ghost.* This lovable pool of righteous ectoplasm helps Christians in a tight spot by giving them the power to jabber at their enemies in lost languages and by haunting the houses of unbelievers until they have a heart attack and drop dead.

- *God's Mouthpiece.* A lawyer, whose clients include Jesus, litigates evildoers into oblivion.

- *Christ-O, Change-O:* A magician has special super-powers, including making pedophile charges against Catholic priests disappear.

- *Beavis and Butt-head: Born-Again.* The teen slackers have found God and now spend all their time at home critiquing Christian rock videos.

- *The God Squad.* A team of Christian superheroes, including Super Virgin, hop into the pope-mobile and vanquish criminals trying to remove the Ten Commandments from city hall.

- *Me and Rapture Pete.* Two junior-high science geeks get a rare opportunity to explore the effects of upper-atmosphere flight on the human body when they are suddenly Raptured.

KENNETH COPELAND

A popular advocate of prosperity theology and founder of Kenneth Copeland Ministries, Copeland recently called for donations on his Web site for his-and-her Cessna Citation X jets, valued at $20 million apiece. "When God tells Kenneth to travel to South Africa and hold a three-day Victory Campaign, he won't have to wait to make commercial travel arrangements," the site explains. "He can just climb aboard his Citation X and go!"

Copeland claims to have been a successful pop singer before he turned minister. He and his wife, Gloria, hold "Believers' Conventions," assisted by other popular men of the cloth such as the exquisitely named Creflo A. Dollar. (The latter, like Copeland, is another believer in "prosperity theology," the validity of which is self-confirmed by his Rolls, private jet, and multimillion-dollar Manhattan apartment.)

Copeland believes the End Times are upon us—or, in his words, "This thing is going downhill on skids, but we're going up." Two of his more noteworthy pronouncements were (1) claiming that victims of the Asian tsunami brought it on themselves by persecuting Christians, and (2) referring to Earth as "a copy of the mother planet."

Like all the televangelist heavy hitters, Copeland's Web site has a "store," in which his credulous followers can purchase all manner of ministerial merchandise, such as the How to Receive Healing Package, music CDs that include the unfortunately titled, "How Rich I Am," and an "Elite CX Baseball Cap" that you can wear into battle against that infernal slow-pitch softball team, the Satanic Nine.

Maybe it's me, but I can't see Jesus wrapping up the Sermon at the Mount with the words, "And now step over to my store! Customized stigmata—your initials on my wounds! You want miracles—I'll show you miracles. All major drachmas accepted!"

Odds of being Raptured: 800–1.

Only chance: if he lets God ride in his Cessna.

Act of desperation: builds spaceship from Popular Mechanics blueprints in an attempt to reach the mother planet.

RICK WARREN

Warren wears paunch-obscuring Hawaiian shirts and a goatee that makes him resemble a suburban grill-meister. As the minister at the Saddleback megachurch in Lake Forest, California, and author of the monstrously successful *The Purpose Driven Life*, which has sold 30 million copies (about one for every born-again U.S. adult), Warren is one of the most prominent of all evangelicals. His manner is laid back and folksy, and he claims to embrace diversity—as long as it's defined as pro-heterosexual and pro-Christ, and antiabortion, anti–gay marriage, anti–embryonic stem cell research, anti-euthanasia, and anti–"activist judges."

He aims to recruit "1 billion Christian foot soldiers" who are willing to do "whatever it takes" to turn Earth into a pur-pose-driven, Christian planet. He's off to a crackling start, with more than four hundred thousand ministers and priests in 162 countries. (*Source:* Slate.com.)

Odds of being Raptured: 2,000–1

Only chance: he cuts God in for a share of his royalties.

Act of desperation: he and his purpose-driven army invade Greenwich Village.

TED HAGGARD

Reverend Ted, as he's known to friends such as G. W. Bush, with whom he speaks every Monday morning, is an outspoken opponent of same-sex marriage. Ergo, he was exposed as a closeted gay man purchasing the services of a male escort that included sodomy and crystal meth. He did everything but star as Judy Garland at *Don't Tell Mama*.

In November 2006, Haggard—who the *New York Times* called "one of the most influential Christian leaders"—abruptly resigned as president of the influential National Association of Evangelicals, as well as his fourteen-thousand-member New Life Church. This was in response to the public exposure by a gay escort, who accused Haggard of paying for sex every month for three years and purchasing methamphetamine.

Haggard denied that he'd had sex with the escort and admitted that he'd bought the speed, but that he never used it. (See box: My Confession by Ted Haggard.) This was not enough to convince an independent oversight board at Mr. Haggard's New Life Church, which concluded that he had "committed sexually immoral conduct" and dismissed him as senior pastor. Haggard thus secured a place for himself in the Christian moralist/drug addict circle of Hell, part of an entirely new wing that Dante—who had to completely tear up his Inferno—was forced to add just to accommodate the American right wing.

Odds of being Raptured: you're kidding, right?

Only chance: he has incriminating photos of Jesus and Peter at the Roman baths.

Act of desperation: serves as grand marshal at San Francisco Gay Pride Parade.

TED HAGGARD'S CONFESSION

Ladies and gentlemen in Christ—it's not what you think.

The accusations leveled at me are vicious, scurrilous smears from Christ's enemies. I will not deny that I met the man, Mr. Jones. Mike. I call him Studmuffin. But that's beside the point.

And I will not deny that I met Mike regularly. But the reason I met him regularly was I wanted to minister to one of God's fallen. After all, anyone who sells a highly addictive, illegal drug to a man of God and then has sex with him every month for three years is clearly depraved.

Yes, I admit I purchased the methamphetamine. But Mike told me it was a new kind of Red Bull, that it would give me energy to preach the Gospel. I figured I'll sleep when I get to Heaven. After all, there isn't much to do there. No football. Lounging on a cloud all day playing a harp? Sorry, not for this cowboy.

But even then, I didn't use the meth. I threw it away. It just happened to land in my soup. Campbell's cream of mushroom. So I took it by accident. And you know what? I'm not un-proud that I took it—by accident. Because now I know what it feels like to be under the spell of this scourge of Satan. And tell me: how else can I minister to the drug-addicted community if I haven't walked a mile in their shoes?

CHUCK COLSON

The name is familiar, right? Of course. Chuck Colson, aka Charles Colson, is the former Nixon counsel, Dirty Trickster, and compiler of Dick's enemies list who was indicted in the Watergate scandal. On his way to being sentenced, Colson

Now you're probably wondering: did I have gay sex with this boy? No, I did not have gay sex with him. I had good, old-fashioned straight sex. You know, somebody on top, somebody else on the bottom. I saw him, as Paul says in Corinthians, face to face. So when people ask me did I know Mike Jones, I say, "Yes, I knew him in the biblical sense." And what's wrong with that? If it's in the Bible, how bad can it be?

People ask me, "How did you meet . . . what's his name—the gay guy?" I met him because I went to him for a massage. He was referred to me. By whom? By the guy who happens to own the local S&M dungeon. A very reputable and righteous man, and a member of our New Life Church congregation, as well as our chamber of commerce.

Regardless of what happened to me, I still want you to go out and vote against this proposition to legalize gay marriage in our fair state. Because the Bible says that marriage should only be between a man and a goat. . . . Did I say "goat"? I meant "woman."

Thank you, ladies and gentlemen. Now join me now for the french kiss of peace. . . .

predictably found God and now stumps for the Christian right's political agenda, which has included belief in intelligent design, heterosexuals-only marriage and the "just war" in Iraq.

Judging from the frequency with which rich and famous miscreants abruptly turn to Jesus, one can only infer that all they need do to be given a moral—and legal—blank slate is to intone the magic words, "I'm born again!" Jesus, acting like a mob attorney, springs the guilty from going up the river and down to Hell. It's God's version of the insanity defense.

Odds of being Raptured: 1,000,000,000–1.

Only chance: if God is a Republican.

Act of desperation: claims that Ted Haggard was Deep Throat—"and he knows what I mean."

TIM LAHAYE

In addition to his Left Behind brand, LaHaye has published several nonfiction books, including *Act of Marriage*, which sounds like the title of a crime thriller. If creating Left Behind wasn't enough to incriminate him, LaHaye was a founding member of Falwell's Moral Majority.

Odds of being Raptured: about as high as him winning the Nobel Prize for Literature.

Only chance: God doesn't read.

Act of desperation: agrees to go on book tour of Hell.

UNGODLY POLITICIANS AND TALK-SHOW HOSTS

Hard as it is for a rational person to comprehend, it is impossible to win national office in this country without naming Jesus as your running mate. Many politicians have gone further than paying lip service to the Lord and have piggy-backed to power on the Christian right. Some even have intentions of forming an American Taliban and establishing the United States as a Christian theocracy (and—who knows?—mandating that kooky mandatory beard law that will make all American males resemble somebody from ZZ Top.)

It would be impossible to include here all the Rapture-pushing politicians and talk show provocateurs who have made a public display of bathetic piety. The cesspool is just too deep. (And they all tend to look alike—pasty faced, with khakis, blue blazers and bow ties, like the progeny of Thurston Howell III.)

However, after careful perusal, following are the leading candidates to be the American Mullah Omar.

Sam Brownback

The Republican senator from Kansas not only wants to establish a government by Christ, but also has sought to introduce a bill that would compel pregnant women considering abortions to provide anesthetics for their fetuses. Yet he proved his faith by turning the other cheek and accepting $42,000 from lobbyist Jack Abramoff (whose picture is in the dictionary next to the word *sleazeball*). Brownback also sells on his Web site flags that have "flown over the U.S. Capitol Building" (as opposed to Mark Foley, who on his site sells bikini briefs belonging to congressional pages that have flown over the U.S. Capitol building).

Brownback doesn't believe in evolution, and like George W., is living proof that Darwin was indeed wrong, and that whoever designed the universe was anything but intelligent.

Odds of being Raptured: 5,000–1.

Only chance: convinces God to substitute electronic voting machines for divine judgment.

Act of desperation: introduces bill to put Jesus' picture on the dollar bill.

Rick Santorum

What can you say about a guy who equates homosexuality with "man-dog love"? Who blamed the Catholic priest pederasty scandal on the city of Boston (hotbed of the left wing, you see)? Who claimed as late as June 2006 that he had found weapons of mass destruction in Iraq?

Santorum was labeled one of the "20 Most Corrupt Members of Congress" by the Citizens for Responsibility and Ethics (CREWS) in Washington. CREWS's report accused Santorum of "misuse of his legislative position in exchange for contributions to his political action committee and his re-election campaign." The latter referred to Santorum's Good Neighbor Foundation, a charity he set up to help faith-based groups fight poverty but that spent most of its money on its staff and expenses.

Neighborliness begins at home.

Last November, Santorum lost his Senate seat to not-as-wacko conservative "Democrat" Bob Casey, but vowed to continue his mad homophobic ravings in the private sector.

Odds of being Raptured: about the same as finding a televangelist without a rap sheet.

Only chance: if God is an even bigger homophobe than he is.

Act of desperation: starts campaign to ban "man-goat love."

The Decider

G. W. Bush has declared that God told him to do the following things:

- Run for president.
- Strike against al Qaeda.

- Strike against Saddam Hussein.
- Find a solution to the Middle East problem. (That is, back Israel's occupation of the Palestinian territories and its invasion of Lebanon.)

Hey, George, if the Lord told you to jump off the Golden Gate Bridge, would you do it? And why is it that God only talks to idiots like politicians, ministers, and college football coaches? Why doesn't he ever tell Stephen Hawking what to do? Because He knows that Hawking would tear apart the very logic of his existence, that's why.

I also wonder in what way God talks to Bush. Is it through a disembodied voice, a kind of cosmic intercom? ("Cough, cough, this is your Lord speaking. Will George W. Bush please report to the Situation Room?") By "throwing his voice," ventriloquist-style? Does He appear in a burning bush? ("I was burnin' some brush on the ranch and some of it caught fire and told me that I should invade Iran.") Via Charlton Heston? ("I was playing golf with the Big Guy last week, and he told me to tell you: thumbs up on the Abu Ghraib thing.") One thing is sure: God doesn't give George his marching orders in print.

Question #1: If Bush claims that the Lord is giving him orders, then according to the Nuremberg Trials, isn't God ultimately responsible for lying the nation into an illegal war, illicit detentions, war profiteering, secret renditions, and spying on American citizens?

Question #2: Can God be impeached?

Odds of being Raptured: astronomical. But here let us pray for the Lord to take G. W. Then he's His problem.

Only chance: his Dad gets James Baker to pull some strings.

Act of desperation: admits that the bulge in his back caught during the 2004 presidential debates was God's hand.

RAPTURE: THE ULTIMATE BRINGDOWN

There will be those who, once Raptured, will suffer a big let-down when they find out that Heaven isn't all it's cracked up to be. People like Billy Joe Milksop. . . .

THE FIVE PEOPLE YOU MEET IN LIBERAL HEAVEN
LONG SHOT of the exterior of a theme park.
A sign at the entrance reads: CHRISTIAN HABITAT.
Synth-Christian pop music.

NARRATOR
(voice-over, in unctuous, sermonizing tone)
Billy Joe Milksop was a God-fearing man.

MEDIUM SHOT of BILLY JOE, a man in his late sixties, with a craggy, Midwestern face, chin stubble, and a paunch, but with large arms and shoulders forged from a lifetime of manual labor. During the following, BILLY JOE will trudge along the amusement park, stopping to inspect various rides.

NARRATOR
He was a loving husband and father to four daughters. He was a deacon in the local Pentecostal church and was so righteous, he became the first man ever to write in tongues. He believed in God, country, the right to bear arms, the

sanctity of marriage between a biological man and a biological woman, and the repealing of the estate tax. And yet, deep inside, Billy Joe thought his life was meaningless.

CUT TO CLOSE-UP of Billy Joe, as if soul-searching. Ominous music.

NARRATOR
No one knows when the Rapture will come. Billy Joe sure didn't when on that hot July day, he arrived for work at Christian Habitat.

As the NARRATOR speaks, we see a MONTAGE of shots of the park, revealing various rides and amusements, including the Noah's Ark Petting Zoo; Jonah and the Whale, in which riders are swallowed up by a mechanical whale and then pop out through his blowhole; the Last Supper Zeppole Stand; the Secular Humanist Dunk Tank, where players throw a ball and try to knock a sociology professor from Berkeley out of a cage and into a tank of frigid water; *The Passion of the Christ*, a re-creation of the Via Dolorosa where an actor playing Jesus is kicked and spat upon by Roman soldiers before being "nailed" to a cross that is raised by a hydraulic motor. Bystanders drink Slurpies and eat hot dogs, etc. All the signs in the park are in both English and ancient Hebrew. Several CHILDREN, unimpressed by JESUS, pelt him with Mr. Softie cones.

CUT TO CLOSE-UP of Jesus' anguished face, lifted toward the Heavens, as the cones hit him.

JESUS
(sotto voce, to kids)
You rotten bastards! Those have cookie dough!

NARRATOR
Billy Joe was quality-control inspector for all the rides, and
personally operated the Rapturama, a ride that rapidly cata-
pulted its passengers in vertical cages several thousand feet in
the air to simulate the ascension of God's chosen to Heaven.

We see riders screaming, excited, terrified.

NARRATOR
In ten years, the Rapturama had never experienced a
problem, until that day. Then as the cars were at their apex,
a cable broke. At first, only Billy Joe noticed it.

We see the shredded cable. CUT TO CLOSE-UP of Billy Joe's
panicked face.

NARRATOR
He tried to warn people.

BILLY JOE
Stop the car! No! *(in slow motion)* No-o-o-o-o!

We see the untethered car careening to the ground.

NARRATOR
He saw that the car was about to fall—on a PBS camera

crew making a documentary for the godless liberal media.
And so Billy Joe did the one thing in this situation that he
had trained all his life to do: he ducked. The car fell and
crushed the heathen blue-staters. . . .

Then, suddenly, came the Rapture, and Billy Joe found himself shooting up into the sky, naked and embarrassed as hell
at his beer gut and pear-shaped body. He looked around at
the other 143,999 "sealed" Christians, also in their birthday
suits. He was disappointed—the Rapture kind of resembled
a nudie show his brother-in-law dragged him to once in
Corpus Christi.

BILLY JOE floats through a long tunnel with a white light at
the end of it. The pearly gates!

BILLY JOE
I'm coming, Jesus!

He is stopped by a red velvet rope. Angelic limos are double
parked outside. Out of them step the following: V. I. Lenin,
a pitchfork-wielding Satan, and Motley Crüe (identified by
the band's name on their jackets). A MAITRE D' whisks open
the velvet rope with a flourish, letting them in.

BILLY JOE
If this is Heaven, how could they let in Motley Crüe?

BILLY JOE tries to move past the rope but is met by the
supercilious MAITRE D', who sniffs at him derisively.

BILLY JOE

Saint Peter, it's me, Billy Joe Milksop, from Lubbock!

MAITRE D'

(icily)

Dans le ciel, nous parlons seulement français.

BILLY JOE

I don't get it. Can I come in?

MAITRE D'

Se perdre, l'Americaine stupide!

BILLY JOE

I get it: this is frog Heaven. I just have to find good old
American Heaven and I'll be in business.

BILLY JOE floats onward on the outskirts of the gates, when
suddenly he encounters a fat, balding, debauched man in his
sixties who sports a Mephistophelian goatee, brandishes a
cigar, and has a porn star on each arm. It is AL GOLDSTEIN.

BILLY JOE

Excuse me, friend, but do you know how I can get inside?
I'm a God-fearing man, and I'm here to see Jesus.

GOLDSTEIN

(flipping him the bird)

Fuuccckkk you!

BILLY JOE
Who the hell are you?

GOLDSTEIN
I'm Al Goldstein, and I've seen more pussy than Sodom and
Gomorrah put together. Now pay attention, putz: there are
five people you meet in Liberal Heaven. They're different
for everybody. In my case, they were the stars of *Anal
Chalupas.* You hang around and they give you life lessons—
which makes no fucking sense, since you're already dead.
(to the porn stars) All right, girls, let's go to the VIP
lounge. It's Chicks with Dicks Night.

BILLY JOE
Hey, what's my life lesson?

GOLDSTEIN
You want a life lesson? *(beat)* Always make 'em sign a
prenup. Those cunts got every cent I had.

GOLDSTEIN and the porn stars exit. Billy Joe is left to ponder
the meaning of this encounter.

NARRATOR
Billy Joe discovered that Al Goldstein was right. The other
people he met in Heaven were just as surprising . . . his ex-
wife, who had become a lesbian feminist. . . .

His ex-wife, PRISCILLA, appears—she's ultrabutch, wears a
biker jacket, and punches him in the stomach.

PRISCILLA
You patriarchal SOB!

As BILLY JOE is recovering from being doubled over by his wife's blows, who should appear but BILL CLINTON. He's very fat.

BILLY JOE
Bill Clinton! I didn't know you were dead.

CLINTON
Yup. The old ticker gave way. Too many chalupas.

CLINTON pulls out a chalupa from his pocket, bites into it.

CLINTON
Mmmmm! *Muy delicioso!*

BILLY JOE
Life lesson?

CLINTON
(in between bites)
Don't shit where you eat.

CLINTON disappears. In his place is BARBRA STREISAND.

BILLY JOE
Barbra Streisand.

STREISAND
Hey, geezer, come over here! How come there's no Evian in my trailer!

She shakes him by the lapels until he collapses.

STREISAND
Life lesson: don't mess with a diva.

DISSOLVE to Liberal Heaven, a few hours later. BILLY JOE opens his eyes, lifts face upward, starts praying.

BILLY JOE
Lord, I don't understand this place. And that's okay. I know your wisdom surpasseth all understanding. And it will all be worth it to sit at your right-hand side. Just give me a sign, Lord. A sign.

Sound of very effeminate gay man's voice resounding through Heaven.

GAY GOD
(offscreen)
Bitch, bitch, bitch!

BILLY JOE looks up to see GOD approaching him. GOD is flouncing, finger-snapping, wearing a dress and makeup. Extremely high strung.

GAY GOD

What *is* it, Mary? Michaelangelo's here to do the drapes!
The White Party is tonight and I've got to feed two hundred hungry queens. The caterer has, like, vanished, and a
couple loaves and fishes aren't going to cut it! You'd think
the Apostles would pitch in, but no-o-o-o. They spend all
their time doing angel dust! And on top of that, I just
pulled off the Rapture! Do you know what a nightmare that
was to produce?

BILLY JOE is struck speechless.

GAY GOD

Don't just stand there, Miss-La-De-Dah Big Bad Bear Self.

BILLY JOE

Um, Lord. Can I . . . get into Heaven?

GAY GOD
(giddy, high-pitched laugh)
Not dressed like that!

His high-pitched laughter gets louder and louder. DISSOLVE
into Billy Joe's bedroom, back on Earth. He is awakening
from a dream, with great relief.

BILLY JOE

Huh? Where am I? Why am I back in my bed, on Earth?
I was Raptured. Wasn't I? Oh, God, why has thou for-
saken me?

GAY GOD
(shouting down from the Heavens)

Dress code, sweetie.

Two months later . . . BILLY JOE is still in his bedroom,
which has been redecorated with African woodcuts, Frank
Gehry furniture, and lots of chinze and chenille. A
Streisand CD is on the Bose system. BILLY JOE, stylishly
dressed, finishes giving himself a pedicure and places a call
on his Razr phone.

BILLY JOE
Clive, it's me, Miss Thing. So about tonight: first we're
meeting Ulrich and Yuki for cocktails. And what time is the
party? *(pause)* Eight. I'll never be able to put a decent outfit
together by then. And who's coming? *(pause)* Bruce, and
Hans and, oh, no, not that queen! Ha, ha! You know, I
never imagined being Left Behind could be so . . . fierce!

FADE TO BLACK

Why Jesus Is Upset That the Christian Right Has Exploited Him for Their Own Purposes and Tarnished His Reputation, but Can't Do Anything about It

You know, if I'm Jesus and I see Christian Right leaders using my name to pontificate, accumulate power, cozy up to unsavory political and military leaders, exhort the faithful to vote Republican, enrich themselves obscenely and distort my teachings—not least of which is the Rapture, an event of which only the Father and I know all the particulars . . . well, I might be seriously pissed.

On the other hand, where has He been while all this mishigas has been going on? Wouldn't you step in if you saw an entire race—a race you created—trash your good name? And this isn't a new phenomenon; it's been going on for thousands of years.

I know what you're going to say: He gave us free will. Big

mistake. It's like giving your delinquent twelve-year-old the keys to your new Mercedes.

What possible reasons could he have for being so . . . out of touch for so long?

1. He's just not a hands-on guy and can't be expected to know everything going on in his business. You know, like Ken Lay.
2. He entrusted everything to FEMA.
3. He's in a custody battle with Satan, and the lawyers have taken over.
4. His cell phone provider is T-Mobile.
5. He's got intimacy issues. (But it's okay—he's been in therapy for the last 600 years.)

Or perhaps the matter is even more complicated than we suspect.

JESUS—EN FUEGO!

The scene: A golf course. JESUS is teeing off. He's dressed like a corporate magnate on the links. His agent, PETER WOLFOWITZ, plays along.

PETER
This is the life, eh, J. C.?

JESUS
You know, I really miss being actively involved in the firm.

Jesus' cell phone rings. The ring tone is the "Hallelujah Chorus" from Handel's *Messiah*.

JESUS
(listens, then, into phone)
What? My God! *(turns to Peter)* My secretary just told me
that there are ministers and others using my name to
develop their own financial empires and TV networks, and
that they're huge political players. How the hell did this
happen? And why was I left out of the loop?

PETER
J. C., I told you that once you sold your interest in the fran-
chise, you sold your influence, too.

JESUS
The T-shirts and bumper stickers were bad enough. But now
I'm seeing clothing lines, skin care, "Christian lenders." I
mean, first I throw the money-changers out, now somebody's loan sharking in my name?

PETER
Hey, those licensing deals, I did you a mitzvah. You'll never
have to worry about money again.

JESUS
They're extorting, embezzling, and supporting homicidal
leaders who start insane wars.

PETER
Legal okayed everything. You've got plausible deniability.

JESUS
They're gangsters! What will my fans think?

PETER

They'll love it. Gangstas are cool. *(as Jesus looks on befud-dled)* Things have changed since your heyday. Kids are running the show. If you want to get back in the game, you have to change your image.

JESUS

What's wrong with my old image?

PETER

First of all, that love and kindness-meek-shall-inherit-the-earth campaign won't play in the urban market. Or with the gun-lovers. Second, you tried to be too many things to too many people—Father, Son, Holy Spirit. Shit, you had more costume changes than Cher!

CLOSE-UP of JESUS, mulling over Peter's words.

JESUS

What do you suggest I do?

PETER

Reposition the brand. But first, you need a serious image makeover.

NARRATOR
(voice-over)

And so, Jesus rebranded himself. He hired a celebrity publicist, got a new stylist, and worked with a global marketing consultant. . . .

CUT TO: MONTAGE. First, the interior of Kenneth's salon in the Waldorf Hotel. JESUS getting his hair and nails done. Second, Jesus' handlers have him try out a series of new looks. First the traditional Jesus—beard, long hair, robes, sandals. They vote thumbs down. Then various other "looks" are shown— goth jesus, hip-hop Jesus with baggy jeans and a backward baseball cap, and ultimate fighting Jesus, karate-kicking to the song, "Everybody Was Kung-Fu Fighting." The last three looks all get thumbs up from the group. PETER, who looks on during each scene, beams with pride.

NARRATOR
The result was . . . "New Jesus."

CUT TO shots of various billboards that read "New Jesus" and carry a photo of Jesus with a goatee, modeling on a catwalk.

CUT TO interior of ESPN studio. JESUS is hosting
SportsCenter.

JESUS
(to camera)
The Angels win again. They're *en fuego!*

CUT TO: Hollywood Premiere

Limo pulls up and JESUS emerges wearing a Helmut Lang suit with a supermodel on each arm, and is escorted past throngs of fans and flashbulb-popping paparazzi.

CUT TO: SET OF *Oprah*

JESUS jumping up and down on a couch, maniacally.

JESUS
I am *so* in love with myself!

CUT TO: Commercial—party

Bored, apathetic young people clearly not really enjoying themselves. Enter JESUS, dressed in casually hip attire, and suddenly everything picks up. The music gets bouncier and people smile, start dancing and surround JESUS, who turns DJ.

ANNOUNCER
(voice-over)
Jesus. The party has just begun.

CUT TO: Heavenly golf course. JESUS and PETER.

PETER
So, "New Jesus," your Q rating's through the roof. You're *en fuego!*

JESUS
I hate myself. I'm compromising my integrity. I'm going to pull New Jesus.

PETER
Are you on drugs? New Jesus is outpolling Old Jesus by five to one!

JESUS
I don't care.

PETER
Hey, the least you could do is take a meeting with *(points to
the sky)* the Big Guy.

JESUS
All right. *(to the sky)* Father, guide me. Should I continue to
sell out just to be popular and make tons of money, or
should I renounce the material world and go back to
helping humanity?

Silence. Then thunder, lightning, burning bushes, etc.

FATHER
Jesus!

JESUS
Yes, Father?

FATHER
Always take the points.

FADE TO BLACK

CHAPTER EIGHT

Antichrists, False Christs, and False Starts

ANTICHRISTS

Contrary to popular belief, Jesus never mentioned the word *Antichrist*. John refers to an Antichrist numerous times in his gospel, although in those contexts, *Antichrist* seems to describe former church leaders who had begun preaching heresies, such as the idea that Jesus was not the Son of God and that the Holy Trinity was proof that the Lord had an identity crisis.

In 1 John 4:3, the author refers to the fact that there are many Antichrists "present in the world," although he doesn't name names. Christians identify the Antichrist with the "man of sin" or "son of perdition" mentioned in 2 Thessalonians, and with several figures in the Book of Revelation, including the Dragon, various beasts including a ramlike beast, a goatlike beast, and *the* Beast, the False Prophet, and the Whore of Babylon. The Antichrist is also understood to be a group or organization, usually the United Nations or a future one-world government. But more often, he is thought to be an evil government leader, a religious leader who supplants Christianity with a system of false worship, Satan, a member of Satan's immediate family (including Satan's lazy son-in-law), or a kind of puppet human who fronts for and is controlled by the Devil.

Most frequently—and especially when used by contemporary born-agains—the Antichrist indicates a specific person who spreads a false teaching and whose presence is an augur of the End Times.

Evangelicals disagree on the origins and background of the Antichrist. They all believe that he'll be male and white. Some, like Jerry Falwell, are sure he'll be a Jew. Others, citing a biblical passage stating that the Antichrist will have "no regard for women," peg him for a homosexual.

Hmm . . . let's see. White . . . male . . . Jewish . . . homosexual. . . . The Antichrist is Harvey Fierstein!

Here is a list of some other people who throughout history have been identified as the Antichrist, by Christians, non-Christians, and the little people in my head (denoted by an asterisk):

- Various Roman emperors, including a resurrected Nero
- The popes
- St. Paul (for subverting Christ's teaching)
- Peter the Great
- Rasputin
- Spuds MacKenzie*

- Friedrich Nietzsche (at least, that's what he called himself)
- Mussolini
- Sun Myung Moon
- Ayatollah Khomeini (aka Ayatollah Assholia)
- Sam Donaldson
- A computer virus (later discovered to be a hoax)
- David Hasselhoff *
- Bill Clinton
- Hillary Clinton
- George Clinton*
- Jacques Chirac
- Bill Gates
- Barney the Dinosaur
- Kofi Annan (I don't believe this, even though Annan once stepped on my foot on the dance floor at Roseland. True story.)
- Henry Kissinger (Now you're getting warmer.)
- Ronald Reagan (Warmer still . . .)
- George W. Bush (Hot! Hot! Hot!)
- Dick Cheney (Bingo!)

FALSE CHRISTS: A SHORT LIST

Jesus prophesized in his Sermon on the Mount of Olives that one surefire sign of the End Times would be the appearance of "false Christs."

Here is an unofficial list of them:

- **Jesus H. Christ.** The H is a dead giveaway, as the historical Jesus did not have a middle initial.

- **Jesus Fucking Christ.** Not only did Jesus not have a middle name, but he was a lifelong virgin.
- **Jesus Christmas.** An epithet uttered by my uncle Joe (RIP) whenever something exasperated him
- **Jesus Christ, Superstar.** The Messiah did not sing or dance, and if He did, he wouldn't use Andrew Lloyd Webber's music.
- **Jesus Alou.** Outfielder for the San Francisco Giants in the 1960s. He pronounced his first name "Hay-soos" and was not the Redeemer. (He certainly didn't hit like one.)
- **Chad Seymour.** Played title role in *Jesus Christ, Superstar* at the Pensacola Dinner Theater, in drag. Mr. Seymour is openly gay, unlike Jesus.
- **Jon Bon Jovi.** His fans are just dead wrong on this one.
- **Christo.** The artist may fool some people not paying attention into mistaking him for Jesus, but the faithful know better. Jesus would not Saran Wrap the Holy Land.
- **Charles Manson.** Jesus would never have had an apostle named Squeaky.
- **Johnny Damon.** In 2004 Boston Red Sox fans took to holding signs reading: WWJD?—WHAT WOULD JOHNNY DO? They were rewarded when Damon helped them win their first World Series in eighty-six years, and followed that by healing the sick, making the lame walk, and reanimating Don Zimmer.

FALSE STARTS

Although one of the proofs of God's existence—the so-called "ontological argument"—posits that He is perfect, the fact remains that He's never run a Rapture before. Like the roll-out of any new product, particularly one pitched on such an enormous scale, there are sure to be glitches. Like car, train, plane, and stock market crashes. Like mass chaos, paralyzed transportation and communication systems, depression, riots, and overthrown governments. So you *know* his IT team is going to be working overtime—in fact, I wouldn't be surprised if He introduces the Rapture in a beta version first, to try to iron out the kinks.

Otherwise, we could be looking at the following scenario:

"PREMATURE" RAPTURE STRANDS MILLIONS OF CHRISTIANS
Heathens Ascend While Left Behind Demand Explanation from Lord

LUBBOCK, Texas—In a mystifying event, an "extremely premature" Rapture seems to have taken place all across mid-America, say leaders of the Christian Coalition. This inexplicable occurrence led to the ascendance of thousands of non-Christians to Heaven, while millions of Jesus' followers were left behind. The Rapture played havoc with air traffic controllers and NASA satellite tracking, and in some cases left people half-Raptured—they ended up in trees or stuck in the roofs of their homes, with only their heads sticking out. One Missouri man was killed when he collided with a United Airlines flight bound for Phoenix. According to the latest tally by the Christian Coalition, 2,375 people in twenty-nine states abruptly took off into the skies "as if sucked up by a giant Dust Buster."

While initially Christians were ecstatic, their fervor soon turned to openmouthed disbelief when they discovered that none of those Raptured were evangelicals.

Among the Raptured were Jews, atheists, Wiccans, and Dan Rather. "Not one born-again," bemoaned Jerry Falwell. "This better be Satan's doing, or the Lord's going to be on the hot seat." In a hastily arranged press conference, Pat Robertson said that while the event seems baffling to believers, he was sure that "God was just doing a test run, and he didn't want to risk any of the faithful."

However, other evangelicals believe that the event may have been a "cosmic snafu," perhaps caused by faulty accounting of the number of Jews in the Holy Land necessary to trigger the Rapture. Most fundamentalists Left Behind were livid; many sent angry e-mails to Heaven. Darryl Gumm, a prison guard in Americas, Kansas, said, "He took people who believed in evolution and stem-cell research, and I'm still stuck here with a humongous mortgage." Some Christians were more resigned to being passed over, and a few even looked on the Rapture as an opportunity. Vickie Sue Splay of nearby Bushton said, "Sure, my neighbors gone up to meet Jesus, but I'm takin' their TiVo."

CHAPTER NINE

How to Get Raptured, the Multicultural Rapture, What to Pack for the Rapture, and How to Make Sure You Get Left Behind

Some of you may still be up in the air about whether to try for Rapture-hood or be Left Behind. This chapter will give you some practical tips regardless of what road you choose.

IF YOU DECIDE TO BE RAPTURED

Everyone has been led to believe that the Rapture will be immediate and instantaneous. A sort of cosmic prestidigitation. One moment you're out protesting metrosexual marriage, and the next you're seated at the right hand of the Father, stammering, "A hummanahummana . . ."

But what if it's not? What if the trip takes a lot longer than people think?

And sure, God may be all-powerful, but what if he's one of these "visionary CEO" types who can't be bothered with process, with the thousand-and-one details of the Rapture? Then who's in charge? I'll tell you who—a bunch of middle-managers with name tags that read, "Hi, I'm Bob, from personnel."

Getting Raptured may be like boarding a plane with millions of passengers. Which means if you think the waits at LaGuardia are long. . . . (In fact, some Rapturologists believe that God initially intended to Rapture people one at a time, but was talked out of it by one of his angels, who predicted that it would engender petty, envious, "Hey, I was ahead of you in line" type of behavior. The last thing the Lord needs is to have fights breaking out during the Rapture.)

To make things worse, as in any huge, bureaucratic enterprise, mistakes will be made. As you read in the preceding chapter, some people will be mistakenly Raptured while others are Left Behind by accident. (They will try to collect on their Rapture insurance, but Mutual of Omaha will turn down their claims, stating that their entire policy falls under the "act of God" proviso.)

And even if the whole shebang is impeccably stage managed, there is a numbers problem. In the United States alone, there are at least 40 million evangelicals—plus millions of other Protestants and Catholics—who believe in the Rapture. But only 144,000 will be airborne. Ergo, even believers have about as good a chance of being Raptured as they do of winning the top prize at Scratch-and-Match Lotto.

As a public service, we now offer some tips.

HOW TO INCREASE YOUR CHANCES OF BEING RAPTURED

It's not enough to profess belief in the Lord, attend church regularly, and be a proud Ditto-Head. That's just the minimum Rapture criteria.

Think of God as a cosmic college-admissions officer who wants to see evidence of exceptional ability and drive among prospective candidates. You've got to think of ways to distinguish yourself from the competition. Everybody's been born again. You be born again *twice*. Or even three times.

Also, the Lord has a weakness for redeeming sinners. Think Paul of Tarsus, the Prodigal Son, or G. W. It won't hurt to be in rehab, like Rush, or Gamblers Anonymous, like Bill Bennett.

Solicit a letter of recommendation from your local pastor (better yet, from a heavy evangelical hitter—say, Rick Warren).

The letter should read like as follows (*Tip:* It should not begin: "To Whom It May Concern"):

Dear Lord:

I am writing to you to recommend the Rapture of *[your name]*. As minister of the First Church of the Holy Spirit here in Biloxi, I have had the privilege of knowing and working with [your name]. He has helped me to build a strong Christian community. As proof, our revenues increased 15.6% in 2006, and our flag football team pummeled the Second Church of the Holy Spirit, 38–6.

I realize that before *[your name]* was come unto you, Lord, *[your name]* was a major-league sinner.

But *[your name]* has realized the error of his ways, settled the victims' civil suit, done community service, and wears his GPS ankle bracelet, well, religiously.

He doesn't like to brag about his faith, but I would be remiss if I didn't list a few of his many accomplishments as a warrior of Christ:

- Leads a purpose-driven life (although he once confided in me that he didn't know what the purpose was).
- Consistently voted against gay marriage amendment.
- Arranged special midnight audience participation screenings of *The Passion of the Christ,* and dressed up as Caiphus, in a toga and everything.
- Put boxer shorts on the nude statue of David in the city hall vestibule.
- Justifiably berated another member of our congregation, Ronnie Stumpf, for pretending to speak in tongues while actually being an auctioneer.
- Developed secret born-again handshake for members of our congregation.
- Proudly wears I'M WITH JESUS T-shirt, with arrow pointing not at STUPID, but straight up at you.
- "Tricks" non-Christian kids at Halloween.

Something like that should do the trick. But just to make sure, attach any documents or photos you think would bolster your case. I'm talking SAT scores, photos of you and the Pope or Frank Sinatra, and an essay—no more than five hundred words—explaining why you are the right person to be Raptured. (For more tips, see box: How to Get on the Rapture A List.)

HOW TO GET ON THE RAPTURE A LIST

- Make friends with the bouncer.

- Buy Tom Emanski's *How to Get Raptured* instructional DVD.

- Take flying lessons.

- While praying to God at night, pass along incriminating information about your fellow parishioners.

- Don't just speak in tongues, but rap in them (e.g., "money, cash, hos" sounds great in ancient Aramaic).

- Use reverse psychology: tell the Lord "I'm not worthy of being Raptured."

- Bribe an angel.

- Tell the doorman "I'm with Madonna."

- Guys, bring a woman.

- If all else fails, make a deal with the Devil. Hey, how bad do you want it?

WHAT TO PACK FOR THE RAPTURE

- Two forms of ID, including heavenly passport

- Bible (counts as one form of ID)

- Disposable camera

- PowerBar

- Carry-on luggage

- GPS wristwatch

- Oxygen mask

- Headphones (for the in-flight movie)

- Something to read during "processing" (see Bible)

- An attorney (just in case)

- Clean underwear—no bikini briefs, thongs, or anything with the label $2^{(x)}$ist

- Traveler's checks (for the gift shop)

- Purell (Hey, you never know if you'll have to pass through Limbo.)

- Cash in small bills (to help angels "expedite" your processing)

- Change (to tip the harpists)

WHAT NOT TO PACK

- Body art (especially not the mark of the beast)

- Ticket stub from Black Sabbath concert

- Nonkosher salami

- Any book by Paul Krugman

- T-shirts that read I BRAKE FOR TRANSGENDERED!

- Berets (God can't stand the French.)

RAPTURE IN-FLIGHT MOVIES

The Rapture is supposed to happen in the blink of an eye, but what airline can actually accomplish that? In fact, the actual aerial ride may take as long as Continental's Ft. Lauderdale to Portland route, with stopovers. But that's okay, because while American airlines have cut passenger amenities to the bone, the Chosen are different. There will be pillows, snacks (well, mostly beer nuts), and in-flight movies. We've obtained the list of the latter:

- *Armageddon*
- *Earthquake* (Also: *The Day After Tomorrow, Twister,* and *Titanic.* God loves disaster flicks, and has been heard in his screening room to utter things like, "You call *that* a tsunami?")
- *The World Is Not Enough*
- *Gone with the Wind*

- *Die Another Day*
- *The Devil Wears Prada*
- *Herbie—Fully Loaded*
- *Big Momma's House 2*
- *Up Yours, Harry Potter*
- *Snakes on a Plane*

MULTICULTURAL RAPTURE

What many Rapture scholars haven't taken into account is the possibility that the Lord may want to hold multiple Raptures or that the Rapture experience will differ according to the Rapturee's social and ethnic background. This is the theory of the multicultural Rapture, and here is a breakdown of what a customized, politically correct Rapture would look like, with the cosmological ramifications of being Raptured and being Left Behind.

Italian Rapture
Raptured: For the rest of eternity, you get to have home-cooked meals and live with your mother. Women are forever virgins.
Left Behind: You must spend the rest of eternity at the Olive Garden, with your face perpetually sunk into the pasta trough.

Irish Rapture
Raptured: No guilt.
Left Behind: BYOB.

German Rapture
Raptured: You get to organize Heaven.
Left Behind: You must wear lederhosen and play in an oompah band for at least the next five millennia.

Latino Rapture
Raptured: Spanish spoken in Heaven
Left Behind: Satan uses you as a piñata.

Liberal Rapture
Raptured: Hell NIMBY
Left Behind: You're NRA target practice.

Japanese Rapture
Raptured: You get to take as many photographs of Heaven as you like.
Left Behind: You are scapegoated by the fallen and forced to eat *fugu* "fresh from the sea."

Redneck Rapture
Raptured: You get to marry all the cousins you want.
Left Behind: You must live under John Kerry administration for the rest of time.

Chinese Rapture
Raptured: Heaven is decorated according to feng shui.
Left Behind: Hell is decorated with same scheme used by One Hung Lo restaurant.

Foodie Rapture
Raptured: Jean-Georges runs the heavenly restaurant, and you always have a table reserved.
Left Behind: Chunks of you are mixed into the cookie dough at Stone Cold Creamery.

African-American Rapture
Raptured: You are ushered up to Heaven on the Soul Train.
Left Behind: You must spend the rest of eternity handcuffed to Al Sharpton.

Gay Rapture
Raptured: You get to see the look on the faces of the other Christians.
Left Behind: You must shop at Sam's Club.

Highly Sensitive People (HSP) Rapture
Raptured: God gives you a hearty handshake and tells you that he, too, is a HSP.
Left Behind: Passive-aggressive demons undermine your self-esteem . . . and it just never stops.

People in Therapy Rapture
Raptured: You fly up to Heaven on your couch; your therapist is Left Behind.
Left Behind: Your shrink tells you that eternal damnation is just another "life lesson—just a very long one."

Celebrity Rapture
Raptured: Oprah is a guest on *your* show.
Left Behind: You're named cohost of *Abscess Hollywood*.

HOW TO ENSURE THAT YOU'RE LEFT BEHIND
Human beings are funny. They often do things that they know are knuckleheaded, like vote against their best interests or videotape their bachelor party and put it on the Internet. Even though they know that being Left Behind will be the

ultimate nightmare, there will be some hardcore sinners who even if given a blanket amnesty by the Almighty, still would prefer to stay here on the planet of the damned.

We've interviewed many of these irredeemable losers and from their responses we've compiled their reasons for wanting to be Left Behind, as well as some tips on how to ensure that.

SIX BEST REASONS FOR WANTING TO BE LEFT BEHIND

1. 144,000 more job openings (although most of them will be at Wal-Mart)
2. 144,000 more parking spaces (extra large, since most of the Raptured drive SUVs)*
3. 144,000 more SUVs
4. Many more vacant, fully furnished homes and apartments.
5. 144,000 fewer Republican voters
6. 144,000 wardrobes (unfortunately, they're all size 50)

HOW TO ENSURE THAT YOU'RE LEFT BEHIND

- Join the Man-Boy Love Association.
- Open an "Abortion on Demand" stand at the county fair.
- Display ROB REINER FOR PRESIDENT bumper sticker.
- Be caught wishing people "Happy Holidays" instead of "Merry Christmas."*
- Worship the golden calf on your patio.
- Be discovered with a copy of *Marx for Dummies*.
- On the day of the Rapture, dress up as Liza Minnelli.

*Courtesy of Stephany Evans.

CHAPTER TEN

The Rapture—God's Greatest Product Launch

There's no getting around it: the Rapture is going to scare the bejeezus out of people. (No pun intended.) Especially if it happens in the "twinkling of an eye," as Paul promises in his letter to the Corinthians. Which means no invitation, no warning—nothing. Just boom!—out of the blue. You're here one minute and gone the next.

God's a spontaneous dude.

And a lot of people aren't going to like it. They'll be a sizable opposition. People will call it another Vietnam. Or Rapturegate.

In fact, God himself hasn't been polling very well. The only issue on which the public supports Him is the war on Satanic terror. So if he wants to get away with the wholesale disappearance of thousands, if not millions, of people, plus a world wracked with war, famine, pestilence, and flying dragons, he'd better have a killer public-relations campaign.

God knows this; He isn't stupid. In fact, he's hired Karl Rove to direct his campaign strategy and Howard Rubenfeld, CEO of Gutless and Rubenfeld, one of the world's largest PR firms, whose other clients include Kim Jong-Il, Donald Rumsfeld, and four of the nation's top-five serial killers. Rubenfeld likes to call himself "the Lord's flack," and generally keeps a tight lid on his projects. But through dogged investigative journalism that we've made up, we have acquired a copy of his plan to roll out the deadliest product launch since New Coke.

THE RAPTURE: THE MARKETING PLAN

We here at Rubenfeld and Associates have spent months planning the launch of God's latest and greatest product, the Rapture. Extensive research, including polling, focus groups, and test marketing. [See chapter 8: "'Premature' Rapture Strands Millions."]

In addition to posing the greatest logistical challenge since the pyramids, the Rapture will most certainly be among the world's greatest disasters (of course, it will be nothing compared with the Tribulation, which we are also hard at work on).

We aim to roll out the Rapture in over 180 nations, after advance previews in Sodom and Gomorrah (i.e., New York and Hollywood). We've developed a multipronged publicity campaign, composed of the following elements.

- Announce that the Rapture Index is now higher than the Dow Jones Industrial Average, which means it's time for the End Times

- Declare that we discovered that Satan has weapons of mass destruction, including mustard gas, anthrax, and little red demons with mini-pitchforks that perch on your shoulder and tell you to cheat on your taxes. (Have one of our representatives—*not* Pat Robertson—show up at the UN and wave "photos" taken by special infrared cameras that supposedly demonstrate the existence of the devilish homunculi.)

- Secure the services of certain "average everyday Christians," who will testify that Satan tried to coerce them into committing evil deeds such as cutting in line at the Piggly-Wiggly and harboring unclean thoughts about the Little Mermaid

- Pay off one of Satan's former believers to claim that Satan reneged on a deal in which, in exchange for his soul, Satan would turn him into a superstar center fielder for the Washington Nationals who helps beat the hated Yankees in the World Series while singing show tunes in a suspiciously high tenor

- Get the right-wing talk shows behind us: *Rush, Hannity, Savage, Colbert,* and so on

- Reorganize the Homeland Security terror alert system along the following lines: red—increase in overheard Satanic chatter that could indicate that he is planning to "pump up the evil"; vermilion—possible indication that Satan plans to demonically possess major U.S. leaders and force them to declare Wicca as the national religion; crimson—rerelease of *Rosemary's Baby;* maroon—specific

knowledge that Satan plans to accelerate global
warming, that he wants "everyone up there to
feel my pain"

- Launch a campaign of attack ads against Satan
  and his minions [See chapter 12.]
- Sponsor a grassroots outreach program in which
  thousands of evangelical ministers "talk up" the
  Rapture in their sermons
- Get the bloggers (Drudge, etc.) to pound home
  our main talking points—the end is near; Christians had better get in line; and if you're not with
  God, you're with the terrorists
- Hire the Swift Boat Veterans for Truth to testify
  that in 1966 Satan appeared to their company
  and led them straight into a Vietcong ambush
- Create content for iPods, including two-minute
  versions of the Rapture in which only cool
  teenagers are Raptured while parents and
  teachers are Left Behind. This will help us win
  over the fifteen to thirty-two demographic.
- Write speech spinning the Rapture for the Lord's
  press secretary, Ari Fleischer [See chapter 11.]

We would like to thank our many corporate sponsors,
including ExxonMobil, Bechtel, General Electric, Wal-Mart,
and the United States Armed Forces, which shared its invalu-
able counterinsurgency propaganda advice.

CHAPTER ELEVEN

Rapture Spin Control

In the wake of the Rapture, the greatest cataclysm in history, the entrenched elites—and by that I mean God, Satan, the Antichrist, and the Bush administration—will be trying their utmost to sway public opinion in a direction that best supports their agenda.

God will simultaneously try to take credit for Rapturing the chosen and seek to avoid responsibility for the carnage on Earth. Satan will use the Rapture as an incitement to rally his troops, a kind of Pearl Harbor for Armageddon. The Antichrist will insidiously try to exploit the terrified population and accumulate power by presenting himself as a "uniter, not a divider." The Bush administration will attempt to convince the "reality-based community" that the Rapture simply didn't happen. It will be field day for the pundits. And the post-Rapture will be a great time to be a spinmeister.

A POST-RAPTURE BRIEFING BY GOD'S SPOKESPERSON, ARI FLEISCHER

Good evening to all those of you Left Behind. At 8:13 this morning East Coast time, over one 100 million people disappeared out of their clothes and were Raptured to a better place. To those whose friends and loved ones abruptly vanished, leaving only their clothes behind, including their underthings, hearing aids, implants, artificial limbs, and in at least one case a penile prosthesis—we offer our deepest sympathy.

To those who were injured as a result of accidents caused by this decision—pilotless planes crashing, engineers vanishing from high-speed trains gone haywire, wrecking balls dropped on your head by the sudden disappearance of construction foremen, patients left to lie on the operating table while their new liver flopped to the floor—you get the picture—you have our most sincere condolences.

The rest of you are probably wondering why. Why were you Left Behind while your no-good brother-in-law who never worked a day in his life, and not only that but sniffed airplane glue when nobody was around, is now sitting at the Lord's side sipping an appletini while a chorus of harpists plays Bach and several hot and heavenly masseuses give him a relaxing loofah bath (which up here we call the O'Reilly)?

Well, we do have some answers. But before we get to them, the Lord urges all Americans to stay calm. Difficult times will be ahead. There will be plagues; famines; nucular [*sic*] attacks;

giant, flying, and fire-breathing dragons. Mass panic and chaos. The complete breakdown of civil society. The best thing you can do in such trying times is to live your lives. Go shopping. Stimulate the economy. If you allow the man-eating serpent monsters to interfere with the American way of life, well, Satan wins.

Now, as to why the Lord launched this preemptive Rapture. The short answer is that he's the Lord, so He can basically do whatever he wants, including wage war as he sees fit. This is justified under the legal theory known as the unitary Creator.

Also, Satan failed to adhere to the minimal standards of international law. He waged war on his own people, fomented civil unrest in Purgatory, and forced numerous young children to spin their heads 360 degrees and projectile-vomit pea soup.

God did not take this Satanic mayhem lying down. He reacted immediately and forcefully in response to Satan's belligerence. And He promises to do everything in His power to protect the American people from another cataclysmic apocalypse.

To ensure that another Rapture doesn't happen on His watch, He has had to take certain emergency measures: First, He has pushed through a piece of legislation called the Left Behind National Security Act, which permits Jesus to look within the souls of all Americans. In this initiative, He will work closely with his natural ally, Santa Claus. Together, they will reach a determination on exactly which Americans have been naughty and which nice. The naughty will be slaughtered during the Tribulation to come, while the nice will be also slaughtered, only not quite so violently, but—and this is a big *but*—they will rejoin the Lord in Heaven, in however many pieces they happen to be at the time.

Second, the Lord signed Heavenly Order No. 12,948, also known as the Charlton Heston Act, which replaces the U.S. Constitution with the Ten Commandments. No more activist judges interpreting the law as they see fit. Now, you break the law—badda bing, you get a bolt of lightning up your *tuchis*. No offense to our Jewish-American constituents. God is reviving some great age-old traditions. Like stoning, public flogging, and turning evildoers into pillars of salt.

Third, the Lord knows that an Antichrist will arise who will try to unite all nations, spread international peace and brother-hood, and promulgate the idea that all men are equal. In other words, he will threaten everything we hold most dear. The Lord promises to hunt down this arch-fiend. In fact, He has already printed up posters reading, ANTICHRIST WANTED: DEAD OR ALIVE.

In the meantime, he will work with his intelligence services and soldiers to track down this criminal. And He won't sleep soundly until the Antichrist is vanquished. Until the period of Tribulation is over. And until He defeats Satan in the battle of Armageddon that will turn the Earth into an ocean of blood and in which many billions will die.

Until then—happy, happy!

PLAN B: IF THE RAPTURE FAILS
Secret memo from Ari Fleischer
Despite our unshakable confidence in the success of the product, there is always a slight chance that the Rapture won't come off as planned. Although we have been assured by our IT people, it's possible that the Rapturing might be compro-mised by satellites, cell-phone towers, telephone-switching

centers, or a mammoth Evil Relief concert/Black Mass cohosted by Satan and Whoopi Goldberg. Should any of these contingencies come to pass, we have compiled Plan B, which will reassure everyone of the Rapture's eventual success, maintain the integrity of the brand's image, and provide us with adequate protection from lawsuits.

- Deny all reports of the Rapture's failure; in fact, insist that "we are making real progress"
- Declare: "Rapture Accomplished"
- Give Halliburton no-bid contracts to send up space mercenaries to build supply lines and sell Tang to the naked, almost-Raptured refugees
- When presented with irrefutable evidence of failure, blame Chuck Schumer
- Pledge to "stay the course"
- Declare that to "cut and run" will leave thousands, if not millions, of people stranded halfway between Earth and Heaven
- Try to get a "coalition of the willing" from other religions to help iron out the snafu
- Fire the pope

• • •

Satan, too, will attempt to bolster his public image. One of his first steps will be to form SADS, the Satan Antidefamation Society, and have a puppet spokesperson address the nation, being careful not to preempt the networks' rushed-into-production post-Rapture programming. (See box: After the Rapture—It's a New TV Season.)

SATAN'S ANTIDEFAMATION SOCIETY SPEECH

Hi, my name is Seth Mandible, and I'm here tonight to correct some gross misconceptions about one of history's most misunderstood figures. Hear the word "Satan" and what do you think?

The evil one.

Red devil.

God's number-one enemy.

I wouldn't let my sister marry him.

Media depictions lean toward caricatures of a sinister-looking guy with a Fu Manchu moustache, red skin, a red bodysuit with a hood, a pitchfork, and even a tail. A guy who can't be trusted, who you'd never want to make a deal with. A guy who's only out for numero uno. Who, along with Freddy Krueger and the Wicked Witch of the West, has been called part of "the axis of evil."

We would never allow this kind of gross, dehumanizing stereotype to be leveled against a member of any minority group. And Satan, as a crazed demon, certainly qualifies as a minority—vilified and scapegoated by everyone but a few New Age freaks and the Manson family.

And yet, it is almost impossible to underestimate the influence that Satan has had on the world. While I don't have time to elucidate his every last contribution, I would be remiss if I didn't at least touch on some of his most noteworthy accomplishments.

First, he created evil. Think about it. . . . (I know, it blows your mind. . . .) Without evil to compare it with, good would be meaningless! What—you just fell on a hand grenade to save a mother and child? Big whoop. You brokered peace between the Arabs and the Israelis? Like, who hasn't?

Let's face it: with nothing to motivate them to do evil, people would just pretty much sit around watching TV.

And where would history be if God didn't cast out Adam and Eve from the garden? A real yawner. No original sin. No guilt. Cain and Abel palling around like in a Disney sitcom. To say nothing about the classics. No Homer, Shakespeare, Milton. "Paradise Same Old Same Old"? I don't think so.

Besides, Satan didn't just show up out of nowhere. God created him. So if you're into playing the blame game, well . . .

If you knew Satan as I do, you'd find that he's not at all the sinister heavy depicted in the mainstream media. Satan is a regular guy. A people person. He enjoys a good game of Texas Hold 'Em, and you know that joint in Manhattan where you can get a world-class dry-aged steak and a lap dance simultaneously? He's a regular.

Beyond that, Satan has a sensitive side, which he displayed on a recent appearance on *Oprah*. Roll the tape. . . .

OPEN ON THE *OPRAH* SET. OPRAH AND SATAN.

SATAN

I didn't come here to make excuses, Oprah, but being the Devil, you're responsible for evil worldwide! It's too big a job for one man. I worked ninety-hour weeks. Forget vacation—there was always some wife beater you had to encourage or teenager you had to introduce to heroin. It never ended. I was in the fast lane and couldn't stop. Finally, I just freaked. Broke down. I put Cheney temporarily in charge. You know, someone I could trust to keep things running smoothly. I checked into rehab. And while I was getting sober, I had time to reflect on my life. I went face-to-face with my demons. And I had this . . . epiphany—if I can use the word. And I realized that I'd hurt a lot of people over the last, oh, two thousand years or so. Adam and Eve. Abel. Jesus—you're number one in my book, buddy. And I remembered the oppression of the Jews, the whole Christians-versus-lions thing—which, by the way, was totally rigged—the Crusades, the Inquisition, the Holocaust. . . . I mean, *what was I thinking?* . . . Power corrupts. That's what I should've told Caligula. I've learned my lesson—the hard way. So Oprah, I'd like to take this opportunity to apologize to everyone I've hurt.

OPRAH
Wow . . .

(Wild, manic applause)

SATAN
I don't ask for your forgiveness. But America is the land of second chances. I'm making a commitment to myself. I've got a great new girlfriend, Ann Coulter.

(Applause)

SATAN
Annie, I love ya. And I promise from here on in, to really cut down on the evil. Whenever I get the urge to, say, start a civil war or whip up ethnic cleansing or some crazy shit like that, I just pick up the phone and call my sponsor. Things

are better. I'm getting to like the new, not-as-evil me. And I
thank you for listening.

OPRAH
Awww, let's hear it for the Evil One!

(Maniacal applause as SATAN *hugs* OPRAH, *blows kisses to the*
audience, then disappears in a flash of crimson smoke)

So you can see that Satan is a new demon. In addition to
his public confession, he has pledged to institute some
reforms in Hell. First, to save energy and lessen his depend-
ence on fossil fuels, he's turning down the temperature to
three thousand degrees Celsius. In addition, he's cutting back
on the constant jabbing of the damned with pitchforks, a bar-
baric practice banned by the Geneva Conventions.

Satan realizes that all souls have rights, even the damned.
He's offering amnesty to some of the lesser sinners, like
unbaptized babies. He also wants to open talks on a prisoner-
exchange program, starting with the release of Hitler, Roy
Cohn, and a member of the Bush administration to be named
later in exchange for some Christian martyrs. So far, he hasn't
received an answer from the Lord's people, but he's hoping
he can reach across the aisle and do what's best for everyone.

Beyond these reforms, Lucifer—as he's known to friends
and family—believes, like Whitney Houston, that children are
the future. Toward that end, he's starting a program that
trains youngsters ages five to twelve in pride, avarice, lust,
envy, gluttony, wrath, sloth, gambling, money laundering, and
political assassination. It's called No Child Left Behind.

THE PUNDITS ON THE RAPTURE

For the Beltway punditocracy, the Rapture is a once-in-a-lifetime opportunity to pund, as it were, ad nauseam. Here is what some of our leading Sunday-morning opinionizers had to say about the Rapture.

Bill O'Reilly

Listen up, America. The so-called Rapture of millions of Americans is the subject of tonight's Talking Point. Well, I thought I'd seen everything. I didn't think Americans could slip any lower. But today we saw the craven, unpatriotic, despicable, and treasonous behavior of millions who decided to just check out. They abandoned their families, jobs, and communities to become deadbeat, Rapture-loving scum. They've left behind a country in chaos, a country without a moral compass, where anything goes: No death penalty. Gay marriage. Giant smoke locusts. Hey, I'll bet Nancy Pelosi and George Soros are just overjoyed.

There's been a lot of speculation about just exactly where these sleazeballs went. Did they go to Heaven? Are they in the Witness Protection Program? You know where I think they are? In Vegas, pissing away their life savings, having a medical marijuana party with an illegal-immigrant hooker on each arm!

These far-left moral degenerates have San Francisco values that say it's okay to just suddenly disappear—naked, in your birthday suits, mooning honest, upstanding Americans—and leave us to clean up the mess!

But it doesn't stop with these Rapture freaks. It's up to all of us to hold the producer of this disgrace accountable. Even if that producer happens to be God.

I used to have respect for God. He used to stand for everything we believed in—family values, strong leadership, and swift and brutal justice for evildoers. And I invited Him to come on the *Factor* many times. He was always "too busy." Okay. Fine. He's got a lot on his plate. But with this one horrifying act of total anarchic lunacy, he has destroyed two thousand years of goodwill.

I can safely say that as of now, Lord, you've lost my vote. I'm not with you, and I'm not with the atheists. The agnostics are a bunch of waffling, flip-flopping liberals, so they're out. And forget Muhammed, who I don't even think is a god to begin with, besides the fact that he spits on our way of life. But I am god-shopping. Wotan, who's a real man's god, is looking good. And Zeus; anybody who can hurl a lightning bolt all the way from Mount Parnassus to Earth with pinpoint accuracy—well, that's got to get your attention. Let them fight for my soul in the marketplace—that's just good, old-fashioned capitalism. And I urge you, *Factor*-ites, to do the same. That's tonight's Talking Point.

Moving on, joining us now is Pastor Zebediah Johnson, head of the Rapture committee for the Bald Knob Pentecostal Church in Bald Knob, Arkansas. Pastor Johnson, where do you think all these people have gone?

PASTOR
They're with God, Bill.

O'REILLY
How do we know that? Has God released any photos? And if He has, how do we know he didn't doctor them with some advanced form of Photoshop that only He knows?

PASTOR

Well, no, Bill. There aren't any photos. But He prophesized that—

O'REILLY

Yeah, yeah, He's promised a lot of things over the years. But
what has He actually delivered? Let's face it: He's a typical
liberal. He talks about taking care of the poor, but does He
want to live near them? No way.

PASTOR

These people who were Raptured were God's chosen.

O'REILLY

Does that give them the right to just walk away from their
responsibilities? I mean, hell, we'd all like to do that.
Wouldn't we, gang?

(Tremendous canned applause)

PASTOR

Bill, they had no choice—

O'REILLY

Oh, I get it. It's like the gays. They didn't *choose* to be Raptured. They were born that way. Come off it. They're just
slackers. And who knows what kind of drugs they're on?
How the hell else can you levitate out of your clothes?

PASTOR

Bill, the world is in for some very hard times. I would like to warn your viewers—

O'REILLY

Are you making a threat? Not on my watch, buster.

PASTOR

But I'm not threatening—

O'REILLY

Shut up! Just shut up! *(to camera)* That's all the time we have for today. Join us tomorrow on the Factor, when I'll be going mano a mano with the Antichrist over the war on Christmas.

Lou Dobbs

This is Lou Dobbs for CNN. Tonight on "Exporting America," America lost millions of jobs yesterday when workers were made to disappear in the greatest mass layoff in the history of labor. God is calling it the Rapture, but I'm calling it for what it really is—downsizing.

The vanished workers came from a cross-section of industries, and companies wasted no time in replacing them with cheap foreign labor. That's right, hardworking Americans get the ax while undocumented aliens take their jobs.

And what, you may ask, is Congress doing to stem the tide of these parasites who sneak into our country under cover of darkness, steal our jobs, feed off the government teat, don't pay taxes, and then do a Mexican hat dance on the American flag?

Not a damn thing.

So, ladies and gentlemen, it's up to us to do it. The next time this multinational corporation called God, Inc., pulls another one of these Raptures, we have to make sure that the illegals are the ones flying into the sky—even if we have to strap them to rockets.

Lou Dobbs II (the Follow-up)

Ladies and gentlemen, tonight on "Broken Borders" our intrepid reporters reveal the truth about the Rapture. It seems that unlike the earlier reports, the Raptured people were, in fact, not downsized Americans. No, they were foreigners hired by a shadowy firm known as Pearly Gates Industries, Inc., and registered in Liberia. They were given cushy make-work jobs with full health and retirement benefits—get this—until the end of time. The ugly truth? Every last person Raptured was in this country illegally.

Rather than crack down on these illegals and make sure they stay on the ground in their clothes, the government is hatching a plan to give them first priority for the next Rapture. Unbelievable.

And we can't take it lying down. It's our job to guarantee that the next group of people to be Raptured are 100 percent true-blue Americans. We've got to seal the borders between Earth and Heaven. Our plan is to erect a giant force field in the upper atmosphere—somewhere around a hundred thousand feet—that will circle the globe. And if the government doesn't have the political will to guard it, we'll do it ourselves—even if we have to field an "army" of citizens wearing space suits and jet packs.

This is Lou Dobbs—take back America!

Tucker Carlson

Do I think the Rapture will effect the next presidential election?

Well, since most of the Raptured were in Republican districts and every last Democrat was Left Behind, conventional wisdom would say that the Democrats have an advantage—especially if they decide to run the Antichrist for president in '08. But God won't turn His back on his base. So look for new electronic voting machines to be installed in all confessionals, and fire-breathing dragons to show up in heavily Democratic districts.

This election is far from over.

Al Franken

So I guess you heard about the Rapture. God's mad as hell, and he's not going to take it anymore. At first President Bush didn't know what was going on. He saw millions of naked people flying through the air and thought he was back on the sauce. Called his AA group.

When he found out it was the Rapture and that everyone was going to have to get the Mark of the Beast, he said, "There's no way I'm putting a tattoo of Dick Cheney on my butt!"

Yeah, the next seven years promises world war, massive epidemics, economic chaos, total anarchy, and attacks by giant monsters the likes of which we've never seen before. In other words, it'll be an improvement on the Bush administration.

• • •

Many who will be Left Behind consider themselves Christians, and they're going to be pissed. They may stop going to church, jam their Bibles through the shredding machine, even press a class-action lawsuit (more on that later in the book).

The government will do its best to persuade these people, along with the rest of the terror-stricken public, that the Rapture simply didn't happen.

The "Final Report of the National Commission on the Rapture" prepared by a blue-ribbon nonpartisan group of former government officials, CIA officers, and the Amazing Randi will deny God's responsibility for the millions of disappeared people and the havoc they created, and instead blame al-Qaeda, which masterminded the worldwide disaster from a cave in Afghanistan.

CHAPTER TWELVE

The Tribulation—God and Satan's Lollapalooza

It's one thing to survive the Rapture. But the Tribulation—a period of seven years that occurs more or less contemporaneously with the Rapture in which the forces of God and Satan battle to the death, destroying the world in the process—ratchets survival up a notch.

Whatever you say about God, He's not stupid. He has anticipated the firestorm of public opinion over the Rapture. And He knows that his Left Behind followers are not going to take too kindly to the seven years of horrendous persecution called the Tribulation.

What are his options?

Ask forgiveness? Unh-unh. God doesn't apologize.

Deny responsibility? Not when the paper trail leads straight back to Him.

Nope, His only choice was that old standby that he stole from the Romans: bread and circuses. Only without the bread. And instead of the circuses, bloody mayhem. But, fortunately, his Christians have always had a jones for bloody mayhem.

Yes, what better way to neutralize the grievances of helpless sinners than to distract them with a spectacle of violence? War, famine, pestilence, death—they just eat that stuff up. Especially the Americans.

Another thing: God didn't leave the scenario to chance, but focus-grouped the shit out of it.

His plan for the Tribulation was "revealed" to the author in a divine visitation from God's marketing maven, Howard Rubenfeld. (And if you thought *Saw* was scary, you've never seen a paunchy, cigar-toting PR man suddenly appear over your bed and flick ashes on you.)

Here is what Rubenfeld saideth unto me:

> We previewed the Trib at a multiplex in Thousand Oaks, studied the review cards, noted how many audience members had fatal heart attacks, and invited the ones that didn't to a focus group by offering them freebies to *The Santa Clause 6: Abu Ghraib*. [In which Santa gets picked up by the CIA, is accused of terrorism and rendered to a secret detention camp, and Halliburton is contracted to deliver his presents, of which they only deliver about 12 percent, the rest mysteriously "disappearing."]

Then we crunched the numbers, broke it down by sex and age, and compiled it into a memo for the Old Man. Here's what we came up with:

- Eighty-three percent of the key eighteen- to thirty-three-year-old male demographic loved the bit where the Red Horse takes peace from the world and orders mankind to start murdering each other. Here is one typical comment: "They should use chainsaws and electric drills and put each other's head in a vise like Shemp did in one of the Three Stooges' flicks." Duly noted.
- Tweenage boys felt that the worldwide grain shortage should be so bad that the only food left on Earth is Count Chocula.
- The age thirty-five to fifty-five married women demographic insisted that the plagues only strike their ex-husbands and their new girlfriends/ trophy wives.
- Animal-rights activists insisted that no wild man-eating beasts with three heads be harmed during the Tribulation.
- Fourteen- to-thirty-year-olds loved the demonic beings, but felt it would be "awesome" if they could destroy entire cities with their farts. And while they're doing that, they should bellow, "Your base all belong to us."
- The burning mountain that plunges into the sea? Hold off. Could depress property values, says the people-who-live-on-mountains demographic.

- No-go on Wormwood, the giant meteor striking the Earth, and the resulting earthquakes and floods. Typical response: "That *Armageddon* shit is so old."
- Teens are in unanimous agreement that the "one-third of wicked Earth" referred to in Revelation that will be killed by massive strikes and earthquakes should all be white, suburban "doofus" dads. "Like the kind in *American Pie.*"
- The scene in which the Antichrist pulls down the martyrs' pants before killing them got boffo laughs.
- Eighty-nine percent of all respondents wanted the Tribulation to have a happy ending. Some random comments: "It shouldn't be so Tribu-lated." "God and Satan should have a tearful reconciliation, in which each promises better communication in the future." "The Antichrist realizes the errors of his ways and decides to start a charity to raise money for the billions of people he has killed." "The romantic leads, a Christian woman and Satanic man, should get married and agree to raise their child as an agnostic."

"In addition to the focus group, God will launch a campaign to discredit Satan," said Rubenfeld as he backed out of my room, but not before asking if I had any "420" and scoffing down the rest of an Entenmann's crumb cake lying on my kitchen table.

God's Attack Ad

A major element of the PR campaign is to discredit Satan
with attack ads such as the following:

OPEN ON: Sodom and Gomorrah. Its residents dance, drink,
gamble, and wench.

NARRATOR
Satan voted to support casino gambling in Sodom and
Gomorrah. . . .

CUT TO: Shot of God hurling lightning bolts from the
Heavens and destroying the cities.

NARRATOR
God destroyed both cities.

CUT TO: A husband leaving his distraught wife and
embracing his neighbor.

NARRATOR
Satan encourages you to covet your neighbor's wife.

CUT TO: God striking the adulterous husband dead and
casting him into flaming hell.

NARRATOR
God punishes evildoers with eternal torment.

CUT TO: Bill Clinton as president at the White House.

NARRATOR

Satan supported Bill Clinton for president.

CUT TO: Clinton impeachment hearings.

NARRATOR

God smote Slick Willie.

GRAPHIC: Satan in a Nehru jacket at a disco, with a beautiful blonde on each arm.

NARRATOR

Satan says, "If it feels good, do it."

SHOT of God holding up the stone tablets containing the Ten Commandments

NARRATOR

God believes in right and wrong.

GRAPHIC: Satan's picture, with a black X across it.

NARRATOR

Satan—dyed-in-the-wool liberal.

GRAPHIC: God in Heaven, looking suitably godly.

NARRATOR

God—tough on crime. Vote God.

CUT TO: God.

GOD
(addressing camera)
Hi, I'm God—and I approved this ad.

FADE

Meanwhile, Satan will address the world in an attempt to both blame God for the Rapture "catastrophe" and give himself some time to gather his forces for Armageddon.

SATAN'S POST-RAPTURE SPEECH

Good evening, fellow sinners. Today, February 2, 2013, is a day that will live in . . . well, not infamy. Famy? Is that a word? . . . I admit, things aren't looking good for our side right now. We've suffered a devastating blow of historic proportions from a perfidious enemy for whom human life has no value. An enemy who, although he purports to be kind, loving, and devoted to peace, has abducted millions of your parents, friends, and children and killed millions more in the ensuing chaos. How this will win your "hearts and minds" is beyond me.

You know who I'm talking about. The "Lord." Now and always, His biggest weapon is fear. Fear of eternal damnation. Fear of being shot up in the sky like Chinese fireworks.

But I'm here to tell you this: we have nothing to fear but fear itself. That, and giant smoke locusts. And a star crashing into the Earth. And earthquakes and various plagues. That's it. Oh, except for the wars, famine, unemployment, and civil unrest. But that is absolutely all we have to fear. . . . Well, okay, those rivers of blood, which most likely will include some of our own. Yes, that is something to be afraid of.

Still, instead of fear, I offer hope. Hope of a world in which evil triumphs over good, where somebody goes upside the heads of the righteous and the holier-than-thous eat crow, while the wicked cash in and the evildoers dance a jig of vengeance on the windpipes of the do-gooders. A world that allows each and every individual a chance to realize the potential of his inner Satan.

Right now as I speak to you, Mephistopheles, Beelzebub, Alberto Gonzalez, and my other senior cabinet members are working on a major program called the Evil New Deal that will guarantee all who follow me:

- Guilt-free sex
- A fatted calf, delivered right to your door
- Casual human sacrifice Friday. That's right, once a week you get to offer up to me a brown-nosing coworker or dweeb middle manager—and you don't even have to wear a tie!
- A drug plan that includes crank
- Enough Satan Bucks to install an indoor swimming pool filled with Cristal, along with hos of every persuasion
- Seventy-two-inch LCD TVs in every room. Watch the end of the world in high-def, baby!
- Free cable to go with it, natch
- Oil at ten cents a gallon

This is an ambitious plan, but one that will go a long way toward restoring the American Dream. I hope you can join me as we walk together into a bold, bright future. That will also be a total nightmare. But don't quote me on that.

• • •

Satan is not going to limit himself to a soft-power approach, and believe you me, he won't take those attack ads sitting down. Besides the speech, his retaliation will be devastating and will include a diabolical plan to get professional sports teams to worship him instead of Jesus. Word is he will test the plan on baseball's Colorado Rockies, who have made a demonstration of their faith in Jesus' part of their mission.

The Rockies came to Satan's attention in the summer of 2006 when he read a story by Bob Nightengale in *USA Today*[*] that began:

> No copies of *Playboy* or *Penthouse* are in the clubhouse of baseball's Colorado Rockies. There's not even a *Maxim*. The only reading materials are daily newspapers, sports and car magazines, and the Bible. Music filled with obscenities, wildly popular with youth today and in many other clubhouses, is not played. . . . Quotes from Scripture are posted in the weight room. Chapel service is packed on Sundays. Prayer and fellowship groups each Tuesday are well attended. It's not unusual for the front-office executives to pray together.
>
> Behind the scenes, they quietly have become an organization guided by Christianity . . . embracing a Christian-based code of conduct they believe will bring them focus and success.

[*]Actual story.

Rockies' chairman and CEO Charles Monfort told Nightengale, "I don't want to offend anyone, but I think character-wise we're stronger than anyone in baseball. Christians, and what they've endured, are some of the strongest people in baseball. I believe God sends signs, and we're seeing those."

Well, this was an "Aha!" moment for the Evil One. He filed it away for use when the Tribulation arrived. But he devised a plan, and here's how it will play out this coming season:

June 15: Rockies compile a twenty-game losing streak. Manager Clint Hurdle tells *USA Today*, "God is testing us. He has big plans for us."

July 1: Losing streak reaches thirty-eight games. The team has taken to holding prayer meetings during games—while the ball is in play. General manager Dan O'Dowd announces that the Lord has told him to fire Hurdle as manager and replace him with Davey Johnson.

July 28: Colorado has lost sixty-five in a row. They're the laughingstock of baseball, and ESPN creates an entire daily show of highlights of the Rockies' ineptitude. CEO Monfort bans Bibles in the clubhouse, and the new manager, Johnson, fines players for "not cussing enough."

August 4: After their seventy-second straight loss, the Rockies issue a statement saying that, "After much consideration, we have decided to opt out of our agreement with Jesus, and we have signed a multiyear pact with Satan." They sell the rights to name their stadium to the Devil, who renames it Coors Field of the Damned. The Rockies sweep a doubleheader from the Cardinals.

August 18: Riding an eighteen-game winning streak, the Rockies' players admit that their season turned around after they started indulging in "Satanic stuff." This includes celebrating a Black Mass before each game and adding a virgin to the postgame spread.

September 3: The Rockies have now won thirty-three straight, and every game has been a sellout. They sport creepy new uniforms—black shrouds with the number 666 emblazoned on the back. And they engage in sinister behavior, such as only playing night games, and pointing down to Hell and hissing, "Hail, Satan!" whenever they hit a home run or strike out an opposing batter.

September 19: As the team approaches first place, it goes over the edge. Rockies starter Aaron Cook deliberately beans Ken Griffey Jr., then eats his brain on the field.

September 29: After ten days of agonizing deliberation, Major League Baseball commissioner Bud Selig bans from the game "ghouls, zombies, vampires, devil worshippers, anyone the commissioner declares to be undead, and Barry Bonds." Any player caught sucking another player's blood will be fined twenty thousand dollars and suspended for ten games. A second offense carries a forty-thousand-dollar fine and a twenty-game suspension. The Rockies immediately appeal the ruling. Selig agrees to delay the implementation of the penalties and appoints a blue-ribbon panel to study the issue of Satanic worship in the clubhouse and issue a report no later than 2015.

October 1: The Rockies win the pennant! Thank you, Evil One!

November 1: The Rockies beat the Yankees in the first all-demonic World Series. The seventh and deciding game turns when umpire Angel Hernandez makes a call against the Rockies and is spontaneously combusted by Rockies' third-base coach Aleister Crowley.

• • •

Toward the end of the Tribulation, the forces of God and Satan will square off in a cosmically climactic battle. The Bible says it will take place on the plains of Armageddon, which is some bumfuck town in the Middle East. But the battle will soon spread to every corner of the globe.

And you can be sure it won't be limited to press releases. No, God and the Devil will fight not just with standing armies, but by every means possible, no matter how unconventional. They will even go mano a mano. First, Jesus and Satan will meet for the Universal Boxing Association heavyweight crown, the match all boxing fans have long awaited.

JESUS VERSUS SATAN: TALE OF THE TAPE

	Jesus	Satan
Age	2007	"I'm ageless, baby!"
Birthplace	Bethlehem	Newark
Weight	135	189
Nickname	The Self-Righteous Kid	The Red Menace
Record	218–1*	1,678–22
Reach	Unlimited	Even more unlimited
Knockout blow	Right cross	Rabbit punch
Secret weapon	Numchuks	Polonium-210
Trainer	Rocky Balboa	Teddy Atlas
Manager	The Lord	Don King
Most Controversial Moment	After losing to Pilate, refused to meet him in a return match.	The famous "long count." In a bout against "Archangel" Michael in York, Pennsylvania, in 1955, Michael appeared to have knocked Satan out, but the referee mysteriously took three-and-a-half months to finish the ten-count. This gave Satan enough time to regain consciousness, get off the canvas, go home, train for three months, have an affair with Mamie van Doren, get back in the ring, and knock Michael out in the twelfth round.

*Lost to Pontius Pilate, by crucifixion.

GOD VERSUS SATAN: GET READY TO RUMBLE
After their epoch boxing match is declared a draw, they will
decide to ratchet the mayhem up a notch and sign a deal
with Vince McMahon and the WWE.

SCENE: Wrestling arena. Announcer JOEY STYLES faces camera.

JOEY STYLES
Good evening, wrestling fans, and get ready to rummm-
bbbllee! Before we get to our main attraction, Kane versus
Able, we have before our WWE microphones the reigning
heavyweight champion, Jesus Christ, with his manager,
Judas Iscariot.

(Enter JESUS, *in his flowing robes. Fans cheer*)

JESUS
Thank you for having me, Joey.

JOEY
Jesus, Satan claims that you are neither the Lord nor the
reigning WWE heavyweight champion. How do you
respond to this?

JESUS
Well, Joey, Satan knows that I come not to bring peace, but
with a sword.

JUDAS
He'll find out on the twenty-third.

JOEY

That's right, fans, don't miss it. The ultimate steel-cage
death match between Jesus and Satan in New Haven, Connecticut, on Friday the twenty-third. Plus: the world tag-
team championship between the Apostles and the Philistines.
(to Jesus) J. C., do you have any surprises in store for Satan
when you meet him on the twenty-third in New Haven for
the WWE championship?

JESUS

My ways are mysterious, Joey. But I'll tell you one thing: it
will be easier for Hulk Hogan to pass through the eye of a
needle than for Satan to leave the ring in one piece when we
meet in New Haven.

JOEY

On the twenty-third.

JUDAS

And don't forget the grand prize: thirty pieces of silver.

*(A commotion behind them in the arena.
Unbeknownst to* JOEY *and* JESUS, SATAN *has entered the arena
brandishing a chair, which he smashes over Jesus' head.*
JESUS *collapses.)*

JOEY

Oh, my God! From out of nowhere, Satan has given Jesus a
chair shot! JESUS is down!

(SATAN *kicks* JESUS *in the groin.* JUDAS *runs. Then* SATAN *picks up* JESUS *with his forearm under* JESUS' *throat.* CLOSE-UP *of* JESUS' *anguished face.)*

JOEY

Oh, no! He's got him in his finishing move—the Crucifixion!

(The FANS *hoot and howl, and boo* SATAN, *who drops the motionless body of Jesus on the floor. Then he grabs the mic from* JOEY.)

SATAN

You know something, Styles, this is just a taste of what I'm going to do to this pencil-necked savior on the twenty-third, in New Haven, Connecticut. I, Satan, will become the next WWE heavyweight champion!

*(SATAN *thrusts out his chest and taunts the fans booing him. Suddenly, in rush the* APOSTLES, *a tag team, to the cheers of the crowd.* SATAN *sees them and flees. The crowd roars.)*

JOEY

It's the Apostles—Matthew, Mark, Luke, and John. They're chasing Satan out of the arena! It's Armageddon out here, folks!

CUT TO: New Haven Arena. The twenty-third.

RING ANNOUNCER

Ladies and gentlemen, in this corner, weighing one hundred and thirty-five pounds, from Galilee, the reigning WWE heavyweight champ—Jesus Christ! In this corner, weighing one hundred and eighty-nine pounds, from parts unknown—Satan!

JOEY STYLES

Fans, this is the steel-cage match you've all been waiting for:
Jesus versus Satan for the WWE championship and the
future of humanity. Jesus has agreed to wrestle according to
Roman rules—boy, ain't that ironic?—while for Satan it's
no-holds-barred.

(JESUS *offers to shake* SATAN'S *hand, but* SATAN *refuses. Then,
in an apparent change of heart,* SATAN *extends his hand, but
when* JESUS *goes to shake it,* SATAN *pulls his back, and, the fingers of his right hand under his front teeth, shoots him an
Italian gesture of contempt. The bell sounds.* SATAN
tries to punch JESUS, *but* JESUS *ducks. Each runs into
the ropes at right angles to each other, using them as
catapults, and they meet in the center of the ring.*
SATAN *tries to wallop* JESUS *and* JESUS. . . .
But let JOEY *tell it.)*

JOEY

Jesus lets Satan smash him on the right cheek. The fans are
screaming for Jesus to retaliate, but instead Jesus turns his
left cheek to Satan, and the Evil One bashes it. Jesus is
dazed. Turning the other cheek? My God, what was He
thinking? Satan is tempting him to come over to his corner
of the ring. Jesus is curious. Don't do it, J. C! SATAN looks
like he's going to show JESUS something. Satan pulls a foreign object out of his trunk and rakes JESUS' eyes with it!
The Lord is down! SATAN gets on top of him for the pin.
The referee, Friedrich Nietzsche, starts the count. One,
two, three! That's it, folks! SATAN is the new WWE heavyweight champ!

ARMAGEDDON: BATTLE OF THE BANDS

Another front in the End Times war between God and the Evil One will take place in the field of music, as Satanic death-metal groups go up against Christian rockers in a battle of the bands:

Satan's bands	Jesus' bands
Black Sabbath	White Christmas
Megadeth	Mega Vitamins
Satan's Ass-Kissers	God's Auto Body Shop
Def Leppard	Hearing-Challenged Leppard
Ozzy Osbourne	Ozzie Nelson
Judas Priest	Pope John Paul & the College of Cardinals

MERCENARIES DO BATTLE

Beyond the musical arena, Jesus and Satan will recruit mercenaries who will fight an Armageddon by proxy. One of the biggest battles will be between the Promise Keepers, an organization of men devoted to introducing other men to Christianity, and the Promise Breakers, an organization of men who promise to break every promise they've ever made.

THE ANTICHRIST EMERGES—IN SPIN MODE

The Antichrist first will emerge during the Tribulation. The Bible is unclear if he is acting under Satan's orders or under God's (admittedly perverse) orders, or if he's just an evil freelancer.

One thing he won't be is the village idiot. Don't expect him to come off as some moustache-twirling, Slavic-sounding archvillain. He'll be suave, debonair, charismatic, and diabolical. Think: Bond villain.

After all, this is a guy who patiently waited for his turn in the spotlight for *two millennia,* honing his craft in acting schools and Antichrist open-mic nights. In fact, he started his career by simply observing the real Christ and doing the opposite, as the following table shows:

Real Christ	Antichrist
Visited by wise men in manger	Vomited on wise men in manger
Celibate	Created Harlots Gone Wild series
Resisted Satan's temptation	Became Satan's limited partner
Spoke in parables	Spoke in dirty limericks
Said he was the son of God	Said God was his bitch
Healed the lame	Gave hot-foots to the apostles
Rose Lazarus from the dead	Promised Lazarus's sisters that their brother would emerge from the cave, but when they rolled back the stone, taunted, "Not!"
Threw money-changers out of the Temple	Said, "Those money-changers can change my money anytime!"
Said rich people would have a really hard time getting into Heaven	Preached trickle-down economics.
Walked on water	Walked on mosh pit

PROPHECY: THE ANTICHRIST'S C. V.

Before the Rapture, the Antichrist will go by the name Brad Rockwell, a small-time politician.

When the Rapture comes, the Antichrist will hire a team of the best image consultants in the game, including Howard Rubenfeld and Michael Ovitz, who will forge his public identity as a diplomatic, dignified, and humble man of peace. (Later during the Tribulation, once the Antichrist's true nature is revealed, Ovitz will package him with Donald Rumsfeld and Condoleezza Rice in a Kings of Evil tour.)

The Antichrist will begin his campaign below the radar, running for sheriff in a small Ohio town, and achieve some notoriety when he is able to eliminate guns from the public school system (although not from the Catholic schools, where students and nuns will shoot it out on a regular basis).

Following that success, he will run for Congress, announcing that he is neither a Republican nor a Democrat and running on the "Have a Nice Day" Party ticket.

Once in Washington, he will help push through many bills furthering tolerance and brotherhood, such as one establishing "Kumbaya" as the new national anthem and another creating a government agency called the Department of Good Vibes. He will get the House of Representatives to begin each session with a group hug, and he even will publicly forgive Dick Cheney when the enraged vice president swings a mace at him during a White House dinner.

However, he will run afoul of the Pentagon when he drafts a bill that would merge the U.S. Army with the Salvation Army.

Nonetheless, he will win the Democratic Party presidential

nomination, run on a platform of peace, love, and under-standing, and lose every state, including Iraq.

Undeterred, the Antichrist will use his many connections in the international diplomatic community to get himself elected UN secretary general. He will gain international acclaim when he mediates a successful end to the Arab-Israeli conflict by let-ting each side punch him in the stomach as hard as possible.

It is at this point that the Antichrist will have attained the cynosure of power that enables him to exert his control over all of humanity. During the next three-and-a-half to seven years, he will create a one-world currency, the mark of the beast (see chapter 14), and a one-world totalitarian government, and will issue ever-crazier dictatorial decrees, such as, "No beasts will be allowed to wear the Mark of the Beast."

Then the Lord will vanquish the Antichrist, and at the Last Judgment the Antichrist will strike a plea-bargain deal in which he agrees to drop a dime on Satan in exchange for amnesty.

CHAPTER THIRTEEN:

The Post-Rapture Survival Guide (Including: How to Protect Yourself against Plagues, Dragons, the Mark of the Beast, the Whore of Babylon, and Satanic Spam)

Plagues of locusts, dragons, and earthquakes; asteroids smashing into the Earth; rivers of blood flooding you out of your home. As Hillary Clinton, the forty-fourth U.S. president, said, "After the Rapture, everything changed." America will be more about national security, and Mr. and Mrs. Joe Sixpack's concerns will gravitate away from who won the Super Bowl or *American Idol* and toward things like, "If a giant fire-breathing dragon attacks us, should we fight it with a fire extinguisher or a hunting rifle?"

Of course, the Raptured won't have to worry. But for the rest of you, let me put it this way: the Tribulation is going to make *Survivor* look like *Barney and Friends*. So let this chapter serve as a survival guide to Hell on Earth.

Step 1: Prioritize. Make a list of which calamities you can handle right now, and which can be put off. Admittedly, this won't be easy, with a list of threats that reads like this:

- Earthquake
- Crashing stars and asteroids
- Rivers of blood
- Black sun
- Mountains and islands uprooted
- Fire mingled with blood cast upon the Earth
- Forest fires raging over one-third of the Earth
- A third of all marine life killed
- One-third of all ships destroyed
- A third of all bodies of water polluted when the star Wormwood falls into them
- Smoke locusts, shaped like horses with the faces of men and the tails of scorpions, that breathe fire and brimstone and torment heathens for five months
- The dragon with seven heads and ten horns
- The Beast coercing you to take his Mark

Still, you have to start somewhere. Which leads us to . . .

Step 2: Collect accurate information on the most imminent threats. I mean, it's unlikely that every one of these disasters will hit you at the same time. Check the Internet for the latest meteorological forecasts. Place a call to NASA to see if any asteroids have crashed into the Earth or if they're expecting any to land in your neighborhood. Try contacting the USDA Forest Service to see if the one-third of all forests that are burning are near you. The nearest seismological center may have information about an earthquake in your vicinity.

I know what you're thinking: What about the fire mingled with blood cast upon the earth? Who do I call about *that*? The answer is: Homeland Security. They've set up a special Fire/Blood Attack Hotline; the number is 1-WHATTHEFUCK?

For the uprooted mountains, you might try the Department of the Interior. If you can't get through to them—and it may be difficult during the End Times—reach out to the Sierra Club. Ask them, "On your most recent hike, did any mountains move?" (If you happen to live on a mountain that has uprooted itself, you will probably know it. If you're not sure, call a licensed land surveyor.)

Islands flying through the air? Not to worry. Revelation doesn't once mention that any uprooted islands will actually touch ground. And who knows—you might wake up one day and find out that Barbados is next door. That's right—a tropical paradise with great beaches, rum drinks, and grinning, servile, resentful natives—right in your backyard. They don't call it the Rapture for nothing. (As for those of you living on Manhattan island—sorry, sodomites: you're in the Lord's crosshairs.)

It will not always be easy to detect the imminent presence of a post-Rapture threat. I mean, there is no official agency in charge of monitoring smoke locusts and seven-headed dragons. A tip: watch the news. You can be sure that if a seven-headed dragon is anywhere in your vicinity, you will hear "Seven-headed dragon! More at eleven." Stay tuned for updates throughout the Rapture.

Okay, you've done your homework and you've prioritized. And let's say that to start, you're only going to worry about forest fires mingled with blood, the black sun, the horselike smoke locusts, the seven-headed dragon, and the mark of the beast.

Let's run through each of these disaster scenarios as we move to . . .

Step 3: Taking action.

Forest fires mingled with blood. Should a fire mingled with blood break out in your home, don't panic. We asked several fire experts about this, and they unanimously agreed that it isn't any harder to put out a fire mingled with blood than one without blood. As for the bloody rivers, it's probably not safe to swim in them, because no one really knows whose blood they're filled with, or if it's been screened for STDs. Same goes for fishing.

Black sun. It's like an eclipse. Don't look straight at it. Do I really have to tell you this?

Horselike smoke locusts (otherwise referred to as "horse-like creatures"). If a horselike creature approaches you, the first thing to do is find out exactly what percentage of the creature is horse and what is creature. Offer it a sugar cube, and then ask it a question to which it can stomp the answer. If it bites your arm off up to the shoulder and solves Fermat's theorem, it's not your average mare. It's a superhorse. If it flies, it's a horselike smoke locust.

Another way to tell: the horselike smoke locusts also have the face of a human and the hair of a woman. If it resembles your ex-wife, you will wish you had been Raptured.

How to defend yourself against a smoke locust: you will need a can of Raid the size of a cruise missile. Yes, that's a lot of insecticide, but it can be done. In fact, I think North Korea is working on it.

The seven-headed dragon: There are two schools of thought on how to handle this. The first says you can't expect to take on all seven heads at once, so just concentrate on one head at a time. The opposing school says that the way to thwart this creature is to foment dissention among the seven heads. You might tell, say, head #1 that head #4 has been making snide remarks about his scales. We'll leave it up to you to choose.

CYBER-TRIBULATION AND POST-RAPTURE SPAM

In addition to attack by implausibly constructed monsters, you should expect the Antichrist, Satan, or whoever is actually responsible for the Tribulation (that's right, Jesus—don't look down, feigning innocence) to launch cyberwar.

You know those "computer viruses" we all read about back in the day? Well, now the viruses are going to be real. So don't be opening any e-mail that comes into your inbox with a smiley-face image affixed to it or, especially, the image of a not-so-smiley, actually-kind-of-frowny face, because he's got huge boils on his head—the emoticon for "Help! I've got bubonic plague!"

However, there's a good chance you won't have to worry about cyberwar, because there won't be any Internet, e-mail, computers, or electricity.

Look on the bright side: the Tribulation is a fresh start. For civilization, that is. Because the Tribulation will reduce the planet to a charred, postapocalyptic, anarchic deathscape so familiar to fans of John Carpenter and residents of Newark, New Jersey.

Post-Trib, we'll be scavenging for survival like our hunter-gatherer ancestors in a world bereft of modern conveniences such as heat, water, and video on demand. In fact, most likely we will be reduced to "cave painting on demand," in which the demand will come from the "others" in your "tribe" and to which you will either capitulate or end up as a "nonvegan entrée."

To gain an edge in the Darwinian struggle for survival in the Tribulation wilderness, you will need to know about the following.

HOW TO GET FOOD

If you are reading this before the Tribulation occurs, you should start storing food in advance of the chaos, disruption, and total destruction to come. (If you reading this after the Tribulation, sorry—no soup for you.) You will need enough to last seven years, so don't buy anything with an expiration date before say, March 2020. Still, this gives you plenty of snack-food options. (For example, a recent study revealed that Cheez-Its have an atomic half-life of twelve hundred years.)

You will need to feed yourself and your immediate family while protecting yourself against price gougers. For during the Tribulation, food scarcity will send prices through the roof. (For example, a Domino's pizza is expected to cost upward of fifty thousand dollars. However, it will come with free breadsticks.)

The best places to store food are the cellar, attic, garage, closet, under your bed, and—if you live in a city like New York, with little storage space—in your cheeks.

You should concentrate on staple foods, such as oats, wheat, and eggplant parmigiano in a can (which you can buy from the nearest public school).

If you can't stockpile enough food for the seven-year Tribulation horror show, you've got several options:

1. **Try buying some.** However, this will be extremely difficult, for any number of reasons. There will be panic runs as well as destruction of fields, transportation, and supermarkets. The Board of Health will shut most restaurants for violations such as "six-foot cockroach found in kitchen." In addition, Satan might swipe your personal information off the Internet, including your social security and credit card numbers. So when you go to the bank to make a withdrawal and show the clerk your mark of the beast, he'll say, "Sorry, you're not Jack Purvis. He's a guy in a red unitard with a pitchfork." Meanwhile, you're going to get blamed for a lot of evil shit that the Lord of Misrule does in your name. During the Trib, life will truly suck.

2. **Grow your own.** Farming is always a risky proposition even under the best of circumstances—advanced crop-planting techniques, supernitrogen fertilizers, and fat government subsidies. But during the Trib there will be no crops, no fertilizers, and no government. And even if you could manage to scrap together a harvest, the smoke locusts will ruin it. At the moment, there is no defense against smoke locusts, but Monsanto is working on a giant-insect spray called Smoke Locust Be Gone, and somebody at MIT has an eight-hundred-foot scarecrow on the drawing board.

3. **Barter system.** You may need food, and your

neighbor may want sex. That's a no-brainer. But what if neither you or your neighbor has any food? Well, that leads to . . .

4. **Order from FreshDirect.** They promise that their service will not be interrupted by either the Rapture—"We only hire evil delivery drivers whom God wouldn't Rapture in a million years"—or the Tribulation. Regarding the latter, the company promises, like the Postal Service pledge of yore, that "neither rain nor cold nor sleet nor tongues of fire nor earthquakes nor asteroid collisions will prevent our white truck from delivering your artisinal cheeses and ready-to-eat carpaccio. However: All customers must have the Mark of the Beast." (See chapter 14). Should Fresh Direct renege on their promises, there's always . . .

5. **Hunting in the wild.** Of course, you'd have to own a rifle and know not only how to shoot, but also the habits and habitats of your prey. Moreover, just imagine how crowded the forest will be during the Tribulation! What are the chances of bagging a few ducks or even squirrels? Pretty slim. And then there's always the danger of running into Dick Cheney.

6. **Foraging for plants and berries** isn't a much better option, especially if you're an urban dweller who wouldn't know a poisonous plant from a nutritious one. You might have to hire a personal forager.

7. **Live off your fat.** Most of you Americans—and

you know who you are—are carrying enough extra avoirdupois to last you at least a decade. Just to make sure you've got sufficient lipids to survive a prolonged Tribulation, you can:

- Store up more fat. Double down at Denny's. Wherever you are, keep gummy worms, Slim Jims, and Funyuns within arm's length.
- Study the secrets of eating-contest winners.
- Hire an eating coach.
- Cut back on your energy expenditure. At the mall, take the elevator, not the escalator. Work from home—even from your bed. Take up video games. In other words, act just like your kids.

In general, once you've secured your food stash, keep a low profile. Do not go around bragging, "Wow, I've put on fifteen pounds since the Tribulation started!" or, "It's an evaporated milk festival in our cave, baby!" Statements like these are obvious tip-offs to hungry rivals, and you don't want your epitaph to read, "Perished while defending a case of Vienna sausage."

COMMUNICATION

During the Trib, most wired communication systems will be destroyed. That means few phones, radios, televisions, or computers. Battery-operated walkie-talkies will become cutting-edge technology, and you will have to resort to pre–Civil War forms of communication such as carrier pigeons, talking drums, and smoke signals. And those lucky enough to still have operational computers with intact wireless connections will spend much of their time deleting spam from Satan.

• •

SATANIC SPAM

I

FROM THE DESK OF: MR. B. L. Z. BUBB
DIRECTOR, INTERNATIONAL REMITTANCE
FOREIGN OPERATIONS DEPT.
30 QUEENSLAND,
SOUTH LONDON
SW16 2JE
HADES

ATTENTION: SIR/MADAM

My name is B. L. Z. BUB and I am residing permanently in Hades, U.K., a suburb of South London. I have been buying souls for the last fifteen years (at least). But I am always facing serious difficulties when it comes to buying the souls of Americans. They are always asking me to pay with financial instruments that I am not familiar with. At the same time, the cost of traveling to the United States to pick up their souls is too prohibitive. (There are no direct flights from south London.) And they always get their lawyers involved, and I cannot afford to pay legal fees. Lastly, they are so fat that my transportation costs are through the roof!

I am currently in search of a representative in the United States who will be working for me part-time. I am willing to pay 10 percent for every transaction to someone who would help me receive payments from my customers in the States.

All you need do is make my payments for the souls, deduct 10 percent of the total amount and ship the souls to me via SatanicExpress.

If you have read and understood my offer, please send me an e-mail as soon as possible indicating your willingness to work for me.

CONGRATULATIONS IN ADVANCE.

BEST REGARDS,

B. L. Z. BUBB

II

SUBJECT: Want a date with the Devil?

Looking for a hot date with a Jezebel who will break your balls, completely bankrupt you, and crush your spirit? Go to www.newyork professionalwomen.com.

III

SUBJECT: Make your penis four inches bigger—and make it talk!

Get an erection that lasts forever! We offer the best, cheapest Super-Viagra. Cost: your soul, but it's worth it!

Yours,

Liza Stokes

IV

SUBJECT: Lose up to 19 Percent Body weight! A new weight loss is here!

Hello, I have a special offer for you. . . .

The most powerful weight loss is now available without prescription.

Reduction of 40 to 70 percent overall fat under skin.

Suppresses appetite for sugar.

Boost your confidence level and self-esteem.

Beat up your boss and anybody else who tries to mess with you!

Get the facts about all-natural Demonic Possession at www. chubbnomore.com.

V

SUBJECT: Lenders Compete—You Win!

Reduce your mortgage payments.

Interest rates are going up!

Give your family the financial freedom they deserve.

Refinance Today & SAVE.

Call Satan at CapitalOne.

VI

SUBJECT: Get a degree in evildoing!

Get a fully certified Doctor of Idolatry! Advance your career! Rise to the top of the corporate world! Strike enemies dead!

Go to www.gimmeanmba.com

• •

TO EVACUATE OR NOT TO EVACUATE

As you watch giant three-headed flying monsters swoop down from the skies and snatch your friends and neighbors, you may feel the urge to evacuate to a safe place. Well, guess what? You cannot runneth and you cannot hideth from the Lord. Or Satan. And neither one will even bother using their omnipotence to root you out.

GPS, baby.

YOUR ULTIMATE SURVIVAL RETREAT

Regardless of the circumstances, many of you are going to run like rats from your burning cities and plague-infested exurbs.

You will find that a friend or relative's house is the easiest and most cost-effective Tribulation retreat. Maybe you will get lucky and find your friend or relative already dead—or better yet, Raptured—when you get there. Otherwise, you will probably have to kill them. Either that, or try to Rapture them yourself. Good luck with that.

If you are unable to commandeer a friend's home, you will have to build a cabin in the woods. Those of you who know how to do this are in good shape. Those who don't should've paid more attention in shop class.

HOW TO BUILD A RAPTURE-FREE HOME

If for some reason you don't want yourself or your loved ones to be Raptured, you should take the necessary building precautions. The most important thing about creating a Rapture-free home is building a really strong ceiling. That's because, as far as we can reckon, the Lord will Rapture people straight up into the air. The Rapture will be a vertical event, like the pole vault. There is no biblical mention of anyone being Raptured out of a side door or window.

(There's been scuttlebutt in certain Vatican circles of "alternative Raptures." In one such hypothesis, Jesus will not catapult his Chosen up in the air, but merely collect them door-to-door and frog-march them into a paddy wagon. An even more outlandish theory has Satan pulling a "reverse Rapture," in which he will suck the damned downward into his realm. While theologians dismiss this as Evil One propaganda, it wouldn't hurt to put in a reinforced concrete floor.)

Protecting your family from the Tribulation, however, is much more challenging, unless you live in a Tribulation-proof bunker. There are just too many assaulting forces. That's why we advise you to hang a sign on your front door reading, "Nobody home. Been Raptured. Try the Jacksons next door."

That way, the marauding demons going house-to-house looking to slay won't waste their time. And if there's one thing giant dragons hate, it's incinerating a house only to find out it was unoccupied.

OTHER SURVIVAL TIPS

Even if you succeed in Rapture-proofing your house and protecting it from the Tribulation forces, you're going to have to venture outside at some point. Plus, many of you will have no homes and will be wandering rootlessly in the wild. Here are some necessities that will help you survive the Tribulation:

- **Satan-repellent.** Sprays on easy with a sweet-smelling scent that the Evil One can't stand. (*Note:* Do not buy any fragrance that includes sulfur. That is a Satan-magnet.)
- **Jesus-blinding pepper spray.** If you can't get your hands on pepper spray and He shows up, sword in hand, point behind him and shout, "Jesus, look out—it's Judas!" Then, when He inevitably turns around, kick him in the nuts.
- **An ark.** Yes, your neighbors will think you're insane when they see building an antiquated ship in your backyard, but you'll have the last laugh when the Tribulation arrives and they come begging to be taken aboard. Take two of everything, except gays and liberals. Pack in a couple of extra activist judges. (You'll need them when you start constructing the new post-Tribulation society.) If you happen to live in a landlocked area, put wheels on the ark. Or you can purchase . . .

- **A Trib-mobile.** This all-terrain vehicle can traverse the roughest obstacles the Trib throws at it—from hurricanes to molten lava to tsunamis. Converts into an ambulance, should it not actually protect you from those things. Plus, it has sixteen cup holders! Manufactured by the same company that made the popemobile and the Rapture-mobile, a kind of individualized space capsule made of aluminum foil for people who felt they didn't want to go flying up into space naked and unprotected.
- **Gold coins,** thought to be the only other viable post-Rapture currency besides the Mark of the Beast, of course. (See following chapter.) Doubloons especially will be valuable. If you can't find doubloons, try extracting some gold teeth from local rappers and melting them into coins.

One item you won't need: a Bible.

CHAPTER FOURTEEN

The Mark of the Beast

Don't kid yourself. There's going to be a full-court press to get you to accept the mark of the beast. You'll be told that it's the only method of commercial transaction, that without it you'll be unable to conduct business or pay for provisions, fuel, and Antichrist bobblehead dolls.

You won't be able to turn on the radio or television without hearing PSAs for the mark. One will feature adorable little kids who beg their hardheaded apostate fathers not to let the family go hungry—"Don't you love us, Daddy?" "Of course I do." "Then why don't you get the mark?" (Cut to close-up of Daddy crying.) Another will show a nerdy teenager who, after he gets the Mark, is transformed into a cool kid, instantaneously irresistible to girls. People will have the mark—666—inscribed on various parts of their anatomy, including their privates.

There will also be much initial confusion about how people should pay for the mark of the beast, since the only unit of transaction will be . . . the mark of the beast. (Milton Friedman was said to be furiously working on a possible solution to this conundrum at the time of his death.)

I envision that the mark will be like having a debit or phone card, only it will be implanted under your skin and you'll have to pass your arm through a scanner every time you make a purchase. And of course there will be technical snafus, when the scanners don't work or the mark was implanted improperly, in which case the adolescent doofus checking you out will have to surgically remove your mark, enter the items manually, then reimplant the mark. Sometimes, you will be at the Quicki-Mart for two weeks straight.

Politicians will accuse anyone who resists the mark of being unpatriotic and of siding with terrorists. In her State of the Union address, President Hillary Clinton will urge all Americans to get the mark because, "We are all brothers under the skin."

Of course, the born-again Christians will warn you not to get the mark under any circumstances if you want to be saved when Jesus returns after the Battle of Armageddon. On the other hand, if you were *that* holy, wouldn't Jesus already have Raptured you? Let's face it: you're fallen, a sinner, the Whore of Babylon has nothing on you. So *now* you're going to get religion—after the horselike smoke locust has left the paddock or the hive or whatever the hell kind of dwelling he has?

Do you really want to scrounge for food with the world falling apart around you? I'm sure that if you're like me, you don't want to be reduced to begging table scraps from Beast-Marked people who will condescendingly let you know that you only have yourself to blame. Besides, 666 will be cool. It will give you an edge, let people know you're a bit of a rebel bad boy even while you're totally conforming to social pressure. In other words, it will be just like any other tattoo.

Moreover, membership in the Beast Club will have its privileges. It will allow you to not only run a business and buy stuff, but also entitle you to discount tickets for Satanic orgies, Black Masses, and the York, Pennsylvania, Dinner-Theater production of *Damn Yankees.*

If my pitch doesn't convince you, Satan—in conjunction with Chiatt Day—has a major ad campaign planned to promote the Mark of the Beast, or MOB.

AD SPOTS FROM THE "MARK OF THE BEAST" CAMPAIGN
I
Selling a used car can be a nightmare. At Mark of the Beast Chevrolet, we do all the paperwork. No costly ads. No bait-and-switch trade-ins. Call Mark of the Beast Chevrolet today. That's area code six-six-six. six-six-six, six-six-six-six.

II
Our new margarita-flavored vaginal lube isn't just good. It's mark-of-the-beast good.

III
At Mark of the Beast Webmasters, we believe everyone deserves a high-speed Internet connection implanted under their skin. Only $29.95 a month with self-installation.

IV

There are people out there saying you should take the Mark of the Creature. But nine out of ten heathens prefer the Mark of the Beast. So why take the Mark of the Creature when you can have the Mark of the Beast? Mark of the Beast—accept no substitute marks.

V

The new Ultra-Mark III one-touch control lets you see just how evil you are, at the touch of a button. The Mark of the Beast—ideas for life.

VI

Mark of the Beast story #76: Right after the Rapture I was diagnosed with Post-Rapture Mood Disorder. I wondered why other people were Raptured and I wasn't. I had no self-esteem and lost interest in living. But then somebody told me about the Mark of the Beast. As soon as I got it, I felt like myself again. So ask Satan if the Mark of the Beast is right for you. Side effects include nausea, dizziness, and eternal punishment, including possibly receiving liposuction treatments from a Hoover salesman.

VII

VOICE-OVER: It's Armageddon. You need food and shelter. But all you have is cash, checks, and credit cards.

(SHOT OF desperate young woman dragging three-year-old daughter behind her, approaching kindly old general-store proprietor and showering him with wads of cash and plastic.)

General store proprietor tells her, "I'm sorry, Amy, but we only accept the Mark of the Beast here."

VOICE-OVER: The Mark of the Beast. Don't be Left Behind without it.

VIII
SCENE: a supercool nightclub. A young man approaches a beautiful but aloof young woman. He says something to her and she ignores him. Then he rolls up his sleeves and thrusts his wrist in her face. CLOSE-UP on the number 666. She immediately grabs his arm and they walk off together. We see them leaving the club while the graphic reads: "It's All About the Beast."

THE MARK OF THE BEAST AS A BRAND
Satan envisions that the mark of the beast will become the world's most famous brand, as well as a logo that will dwarf the success of even the Nike swoosh. There will be Mark of the Beast clothing (including a Baby Beast kids' line), a Mark of the Beast theme-restaurant chain (featuring "Fra Diavolo Fridays"—all the deviled eggs you can eat for six dollars and sixty-six cents), a MOB Café chain of nightclubs, a lads' magazine named *Beast!* and a combination Web site and Internet portal called MyBeast. In addition, the Evil One plans to launch radio and television networks that will offer original prime-time programming, including a Western show entitled *Marked Man*. (During the overnight hours, the TV network will offer infomercials for the Mark that will begin with actor in a lab coat saying, "What if I could promise you a simple device you could use to pay your bills, buy groceries, and balance your checkbook?")

RAPTURE PRODUCTS

Don't expect the fact of the End Times to inhibit the American entrepreneurial spirit. There will be plenty of Rapture-ready and Tribulation-functional products on which you can spend your Mark, or part of it, anyway. Here is a consumer guide to the best of the lot:

- The Rapture Robotic Massage Laz-E-Boy Recliner. Why should you be beamed up to Heaven without any back support? Why risk spinal injury when subject to the Rapture's intense G forces? Instead, relax with this special chair from Herb Edwards, maker of fine, totally insane Christian furniture. The Rapture Robotic Massage Recliner relaxes you while you blast off into the upper atmosphere! Its pivoting base allows you to swivel the chair 120 degrees left and right, to better keep an eye on the flight paths of your fellow Rapturees. Controller in the armrest activates Magic Fingers. Comes with new fold-out cup holder. Made of special NASA-approved Gore-Tex fabric that won't burn off completely as you leave the Earth's atmosphere. Batteries not included. (Available from Astral Projection Furniture and the Jesus Saves Whole-sale Warehouse.)

- Rapture-Corder. Save those precious moments when you say good-bye to your friends and family for the last time with this state-of-the-art cam-corder! Special superfast lens catches you as you disappear in the blink of an eye! Built-in condenser microphone will record every last overtone of your anguished cry of "What the fuck!!?"

- Is It Salmonella Yet? Food Sensor™. As we've already demonstrated, during the Tribulation, humanity will degenerate into law-of-the-jungle tribal warfare. In this every-man-for-himself world, food will be hard to come by, and preservation especially difficult. This handheld electronic detector uses cutting-edge food-safety technology to instantly measure the bacteriological activity on uncooked meat or poultry. It will help you determine if those eggs for which you just sold your firstborn are fit for consumption, or if that Salisbury steak that "fell off" a government truck harbors a strain of bacteria that will make you sterile (available through Kitchen Tactician, purveyors of fine cooking implements).

- The End Times Wristwatch. This snappy timepiece features the image of Jesus. His hands not only tell you the precise date and time according to the International Atomic Clock, but also will alert you the moment the world ends. (Available from the *Sharper Image* catalog.)

- Wooden Sticks. This set of fine wooden sticks features branches, twigs, and chips. Can be used to build a fire, construct a ramshackle hut or stab that guy who crawled into your cave and tried to rob your End Times Wristwatch while you were asleep.

CHAPTER FIFTEEN

Post-Rapture Culture

A certain faction of Rapturologists believes that the Tribulation will leave some areas of the world relatively unscathed. Even the most pessimistic true believers talk as if some rudimentary society will emerge amid the rubble of civilization caused by the God versus Satan death match.

So lighten up, people! There still will be culture after the Rapture.

LITERATURE AFTER THE RAPTURE

The Rapture undoubtedly will inspire the world's best-selling writers like no other event in history. They'll be a mad scramble to be the first to depict its incredible events and market the results to their insatiable fans.

Chick Lit: *Bridget Jones's Diary of the Plague Years*
 Tuesday 2 February 2013
 129 lbs
 Alcohol units 43
 Cigarettes 22
 Calories 98
 Food consumed today: some nuts and berries I
 scrounged from the park.

The world is coming to an end. My neighborhood, like most of England and the rest of the civilized world, has been reduced to rubble. Plagues ravage the country, and the streets are full of dangerous, anarchic football hooligans bent on destruction. If all that isn't bad enough, no matter how hard I try, can't get rid of those eight unwanted pounds. Worst of all, Brent Northsouthington, the cool venture capitalist I was dating, was bleedin' Raptured into Heaven just as he was demonstrating a new and virtuosic use of the human palette and giving me the orgasm of my life!

Brent—a born-again Christian! Who knew? A closeted homosexual I could accept. After all, I've dated plenty of those. Having a gay ex-boyfriend in your dating *catalogue raisonne* is, well, de rigueur these days.

And what does it mean to be born again? Does your mother get to have another baby shower?

Ugh! The last thing I want to do today is fight for my dinner with a bunch of rabid maniacs at Tesco's. This Tribulation—is this God's idea of a good time? And what in His name are you supposed to wear to it? A sackcloth and ashes? No way I'm shopping at Laura Ashley's.

Am starting to give up hope that my Prince Charming will ride in on a white horse. With my luck, it'll be the White Horse of the Apocalypse.

The Fake Memoir: *My Life in Hell* by James Frey

On my first day in hell, a three-hundred-pound demon named Smashmouth smashed me in the mouth with a two-by-four. At least, that's how I remember it. He could've been a hundred and twenty-five pound demon named Brice. And he might only have made some catty remarks. It might not have been in actual hell, either, but a metaphoric one. But I don't think so: it's so hot that people are taking their skin off.

On the other hand, it's all a blur now. Because when the Tribulation hit, I was high on angel dust. Ironic, huh?

I swung back at Smashmouth, who broke a couple of my teeth, a few ribs, and either my left or my right arm, then said he would go easy on me if I stayed down . . . and used him someday in a fake memoir. I said, "I don't know. I'll have to talk to my agent—he's two circles below us." He hit me a few more times. Just like that, we were best buds. Which is weird, 'cause I didn't know the dead could have, like, relationships.

I don't know how long I've been here. You lose track of time when you spend your days getting a perpetual hotfoot. The character-building firewalk—I got it, Satan. Enough already.

Satan put me in Circle B—for only the most violent offenders. Guys so violent, their shadow would beat the shit out of you. To get from one Circle to another, we have to pass through metal doors with interlocking teeth, guarded by tigers. Plus, we have to show two forms of ID, one with our photo on it.

Life here is the same every day. I wake up, and some demon

hits me with a two-by-four. Then I go to breakfast, where the cook puts my head in a Belgian waffle iron. Then I go back to my hellhole and sit until everything stops hurting and it's time for lunch. Usually something Fra Diavolo.

In the afternoon, I go to the exercise yard for Jazzercise. Then the Jazzercise instructor hits me in the head with her boom box.

Everybody here is mean.

I go back to my cell and wait until my head stops throbbing and I can think. I think about what I am, which is a drug addict, a sinner, a dead guy, and a Sagittarius.

I spend my afternoons with Smashmouth. He's down here because he shot this guy on the street. Fifteen times. Then he waited until the guy was taken to the hospital, had a long recuperation, got back on his feet, started a new career in marketing, and moved to Florida. Then Smashmouth shot him in the head. He said the guy looked like a guy who once cut in front of him in the line at Stop & Shop.

Most days, I read to Smashmouth. I read him some of the Devil's favorite books: *Crime without Punishment, The Seven Habits of Highly Effective Scumbags,* and *Thursdays with Satan.*

Smashmouth especially likes *War and Peace.* He likes it so much he carries it around with him and hits people over the head with it. He wants to get his hands on *The Rise and Fall of the Roman Empire,* so he can cut out the inside and hide a shiv in it.

I read to Smashmouth, and then I go to dinner, which is usually foul, pustulant mush made from God-knows-what. It makes you want to puke. On the other hand, it's All-U-Can-Eat.

When I'm finished eating, I listen to Smashmouth talk about his upcoming trial. Like everyone else who's in here, Smashmouth is guilty of his crimes. He is not only guilty of his own crimes, but also guilty of the crimes committed by other men in places as far away as Latvia. Smashmouth is a bad dude. He wants to go to trial, because if he is convicted, he will stay here in Hell and not be sent to Purgatory, which is kind of the worst of both worlds. He says not knowing whether he's truly good or truly evil will just fuck up his head.

In Hell, there are rapes, murders, and only basic cable. People check into Hell, but they don't check out. Hell is like a roach motel, Smashmouth says. He wishes there was an awards show for the damned, and that he'd be nominated for Best Supporting Homicidal Maniac.

The other day, Smashmouth came up to me and asked, "How come there ain't no chicken soup for *my* soul?" I couldn't answer him.

Detective Series/Children's Story: *The Mystery of the Disappearing Doggie in the Night-Time* by the No. 1 Ladies' Doggie Detective Agency

It had happened around seven P.M. Mavis McPhee pointed to the banyan tree against which her Chou-Chou, Mrs. Pee-Pee, had been peeing. Ms. McPhee said she was letting Mrs. Pee-Pee pee-pee in the yard but had gone into the house to answer the phone, and when she returned a few minutes later, Mrs. Pee-Pee was gone. The dog had not turned up anywhere in the neighborhood; Mavis had asked her neighbors, all of whom knew Mrs. Pee-Pee intimately because, well, let's just say Mrs. Pee-Pee didn't get the name of Mrs. Pee-Pee for nothing.

"You must find her, Mr. Mbotsu," she said to me. Me, being John Robert "Precious" Mbotsu, head of the No. 1 Ladies' Doggie Detective Agency. "Ladies," because both myself and my partner, Petey, worked in drag.

But this wasn't your typical doggie-disappearance case.

Mrs. Pee-Pee had disappeared at almost exactly the same time as the Rapture, which led Mavis to believe that her beloved dog, too, had been Raptured. "He's gone to join Jesus in Heaven," she exclaimed.

"She better not pee on His leg," whispered Petey, suppressing a giggle.

I didn't believe that pets could be Raptured, and neither did the other detectives, but we weren't leaving anything to chance, so we called in some religious experts. They agreed that there was nothing in the Bible that supported the idea that dogs—or any other animals—could or would be Raptured.

"Where would the Lord put all those dogs?" joked Father O'Pornahan, the local Catholic missionary.

"Well, what about doggie heaven?" I asked.

"It can't possibly exist," said Pastor Peabody, the local Protestant missionary.

"Why not?"

"Well, God doesn't do anything half-baked. For there to be a doggie heaven, there would have to be a doggie hell. And nobody's ever heard of doggie hell."

He had me there.

"He's right, chief," cracked Petey. "Besides, I've never heard of any other dogs disappearing into the sky. Or cats, for that matter."

"Crackerjack thinking, Petey."

No, if we were going to figure out what had happened to Mrs. Pee-Pee, we would have to rule out the Rapture. . . . Or would we?

Yes, we would. And we did—and lived happily ever after. Although we never did find Mrs. Pee-Pee. If you spot a Chou-Chou peeing on your leg and answering to the name, "Mrs. Pee-Pee," please write us in care of the publisher of this book.

Legal Thriller/Hard-boiled Detective Story: *Jesus Is My Client*

It was a sweltering, listless August afternoon, so hot that I didn't even have the energy to boff my secretary, Julie. So I gave her the day off.

Then He stumbled through my door—gaunt and haggard. His robe was grimy and frayed, and he looked as if he'd been living in a Dumpster. His eyes were swollen and his face ashen and stubbly, like somebody had drained the blood out of Him. He was shaking like a jackhammer, the sweat pouring off Him as if He'd just stepped out of an oven.

"You gotta help me. You're my last hope."

"Whoa! Don't you believe in knocking?"

"I don't know what I believe anymore."

"Okay, calm down, pal. Say hello to Jack Daniels and tell me your story."

I poured him a shot but he grabbed the bottle and gulped the stuff down like it was a cold mountain stream on a hot summer day. An eighty-proof stream.

"Okay, that's enough. Now, what can I do for you?"

"You're not going to believe me. . . . I don't know who would. . . . But you've got to, I say, you've got to!"

"Believe what?"

"Well, about an hour and a half ago, I just . . . Raptured . . . people . . . a lot of people."

It took me a couple of hours—and a couple more quarts of Jack Daniels—to figure things out. This was big. Really big. I didn't know if I could handle it. But my name was mud among the LAPD, and if I turned it over to them, they'd get all the glory. No, call me nutso, but I decided to handle it myself.

The Big Guy was right. Things didn't look good. He had

Raptured a whole lot of people, which led to hundreds of thousands killed and scores more injured on Earth. Which is where I practice sometimes, when I'm not in L.A.

On top of the murder-one rap and the international war crimes tribunals that were gearing up, thousands of bereaved families who had lost their loved ones in the Rapture had been cajoled by some ambulance-chasing personal-injury blood-sucker into filing a class-action suit against Him. Compared to this, Nuremberg was like an off day at Judge Judy's. This guy was looking at the chair. And the gas chamber. And they'd be measuring his neck—and not for a Charvet tie.

No doubt about it: It was the case of a lifetime. It was up to me to defend Him when nobody else would. But first I had to get my head straight. So I grabbed a bottle of Jack and headed over to boff Julie.

Heaven could wait.

Cookbook: *Rachael Ray's End of Days Get Real 30-Minute Meals, All of Which Involve Squirrel*

Just because the Rapture has, like, Raptured a lot of people and all this End Times gunk is coming down, I mean, why deprive yourself? Tell those smoke locusts, "You're not the boss of me!" And, sure, you're going to be spending more time defending your little cave or what-have-you, and with all this Tribulation you're not going to have the time or the energy to make three meals a day. But look on the bright side: it's a sure-fire way to lose weight and keep it off! But thanks to my handy recipes, you'll still have time to make some Yummo! meals that include one of my new favorite sources of protein: squirrels. They're cute, plentiful, cook up fast, and are delicious for break-fast, lunch, or dinner. For example, here's a hearty meal that will stick to your family's ribs (and some other organs, too!):

RACHAEL RAY'S CHILI CON SQUIRRELY

Prep time: Depends how handy you are with a slingshot. Could be all winter.
Cooking time: 30 minutes / Serves: 3

1–2 squirrels (adult)
2 tbs. This Had Better Not Be Butter
3 cups of powdered refried beans (just add water to reconstitute)
2 cups Almost Catsup
Whatever nuts and berries you can forage
2 large plastic onions
2 large wax peppers (preferably jalapenos)
Low-sodium salt

Roast squirrels on a stick over an improvised fire. Remove the heads and the tails. Cut up the rest of the squirrel carcass into bite-size cubes. Toss into a bubbling cauldron with the other ingredients. Then throw the head and tail in. Cook for fifteen minutes, occasionally stirring the pot with a wooden plank. Remove from heat.

Tip: If you don't have squirrel, this recipe works okay with rat.

Tidbit: For dippers, use your hands.

Confession: To be honest, I eat chili con squirrely as an excuse to eat squirrels. I can eat one, two, three adults and—well, it can get ugly, is all I'm saying. To help keep my squirrely obsession in check and still feel satisfied, I catch one at a time and put them in individual lunch-box-size bags. This way I don't have that big fat squirrel carcass danger-ously calling my name from the cupboard. If I don't have rodents around the house, I won't eat them. Simple as that.

HALLMARK CARDS FOR THE RAPTURE AND END TIMES

Just because all the laws of civilized society have gone down the toilet doesn't exempt you from observing etiquette. And what better way to express your feelings to that special someone at Rapture time than to send them a Hallmark card? Here are some cards for all Rapture and Post-Rapture occasions:

1. Front message: Hey, don't feel bad that I was Raptured and you weren't. . . .
   Inside message: After all, dopey, it isn't the first time you've been Left Behind!

2. Front message (image of Snoopy): Thinking of you . . .
   Inside message: And your bare ass in the sky! Jesus, I hope I never have to see that again! (Image: Snoopy staring at the outline of somebody's fat buttocks in the clouds.)

3. Front message: They say it is better to give than to receive.
   Inside message: Now that you've been Raptured, can I have your house? How about your wife? I've had my eye on her for a long time. . . .

4. Front message: Missing you . . .
   Inside message: . . . but not your size 48 pants.

5. Front message: Sorry about that plane that crashed into your house because the pilot was Raptured. . . .
   Inside message: Look on the bright side . . . er, there is no bright side. Your family was killed, your house destroyed. You weren't even insured.

Sorry, I shouldn't have sent this card. Forget it ever happened.

THE TRIBULATION WILL BE TELEVISED

The End Times, while raining horror on much of the world, will make great raw material for the television industry. News shows will feed on its unending disasters, and more than one station will change its programming to "All Tribulation—All the Time." Wolf Blitzer will become embedded with the forces of Christ, and Geraldo will scoop everybody when he discovers what's in Satan's vault.

Networks will also bank on the Rapture and Tribulation to propel their prime-time lineups. The highest-rated shows will be:

- *CSI: Sodom*
- *Old Testament Idol* ("And the winner is . . . Baal!")
- *Dancing with Whoever's Left*
- *Two-and-a-Half Prophets*
- *CSI: Gomorrah*
- *Mark of the Beast: Extreme Makeover*
- *Devil May Care* (See chapter 19.)

END-TIMES SPORTS

The major professional sports leagues will be disrupted by the Rapture and the Tribulation. For example, the World Series will end in chaos as a Christian batter will hit the winning home run in the deciding seventh game, but he'll be Raptured before he finishes rounding the bases. Instant replays will prove inconclusive, and Bud Selig will declare the result a tie.

A Super Bowl game between the Carolina Panthers and the New Orleans Saints will be disputed: the entire Saints team will be suddenly Raptured, one of the Saints will block a field goal attempt from fifty feet in the air, and the zebras will be left open-mouthed, their whistles dangling from their heathen necks.

MUSIC

Pop music, too, will revolve around the Apocalypse, with troubadours penning endless Tribulation-themed tunes such as Britney Spears and J-Lo's crossover hit, "End Times Mambo!" The new rapper Ludachrist will make a stunning debut with "I Thought You Was a Ho, So How Come They Raptured Yo Ass?" Satan will challenge Ludachrist with his hip-hop single: "Motherfucker, You Think You Bad? You Don't Know Bad—I Know Bad!"

Toby Keith, who will be disconsolate about being Left Behind, will release a truckers' favorite called, "Jes Yer Clothes Where My Heart Used to Be."

On the celestial front, both God and Satan feel that music is an important part of their lives, and will publish their favorite songs in an attempt to win over disciples during the Final Days.

GOD'S TOP TEN (WHICH HE WILL LISTEN TO ON A USED SONY WALKMAN)

1. Handel's *Messiah*
2. Mantovanni's "Music to Be Crucified By"
3. "Funkmaster Jesus" by Pope Benedict XVI & Vatican Funkadelic
4. *The Best of Glenn Miller*

5. "The Rap on the Mount" by Notorious J. C.
6. *NPR's Greatest Hits*
7. *Jesus, the Chairman of the Board: Songs for Swingin' Christians*
8. "Meet the Paraclete" by Yanni
9. *Gospel Karaoke*
10. *Jesus Christ, Superstar*

SATAN'S LATEST IPOD SHUFFLE
1. "Sympathy for the Devil" by the Rolling Stones
2. Bach's *Black Mass in A Minor*
3. "I Dismember Mama" by Chainsaw Massacre (American death metal)
4. "Worship the Goat" by Worship the Goat (U.K. death metal)
5. *A Charlie Brown Satanic Ritual Murder*
6. "I Will Make an Electric Storm in Your Brains" by Black Pelmeni (Russian death metal)
7. *Satan Is Real* by the Louvin Brothers
8. "No, Thee Get Behind Me!" by Venom
9. "Dark Rabbi" by Schlomo Moscowitz and His Klezmeteers
10. Theme Song to *Mr. Ed* played backward

FOOD
As we have seen, during the Tribulation, much of the world's population will suffer food shortages. However, we have gotten word from our local seer that both Jesus and Satan will be holding Last Suppers—Jesus's second, Satan's first. Here's what they will be dining on:

Jesus's Last (Vegan) Supper
Tofurkey
Sprouted loaves and fishlike sticks
Soysage
Not Dogs
Matzos from Heaven
Chaff
No dessert. Dessert is for heathens.
(Advice to the apostles: eat a full meal before attending.)

Satan's Last Supper
"Sabayon" of Pearl Tapioca with Island Creek Oyters
    and Russian Sevruga Caviar
Pumpkin gnocchi
Braised veal cheeks
Eye of newt
Nova Scotia lobster "Cuit Sous Vide" (with Apple-
wood smoked bacon chip, ragoût of French green
lentils, and glazed chestnuts)
Virgin, human, female

KID CULTURE–RAPTURE DOLLS
Toy and doll makers will also capitalize on the Rapture and
the Tribulation, and it's quite possible we'll see items such as
these arriving on department store shelves:

1. *Baby Rapture.* Press its remote control, and it tries
   to fly off into Heaven. Warning: Do not use indoors.
   May ricochet off ceiling and impale your child.

2. *Mr. Scratch.* This lifelike devil doll is perfect for Christian kids—they can pit him against Babbling Jesus (see below) in a match to the death—and it's also a great gift idea for their Satan-worshipping neighbors. Pull Satan's tail and he says things like, "Be my succubus!" and "I *love* Hillary Clinton!" All in a really creepy voice that will scare the pants off youngsters of all religions.

3. *Babbling Jesus.* This battery-operated, talking Christ doll does it all: press his stigmata and he starts quoting Scripture like "Blessed are the people who buy me"; put him in the bathtub and watch him walk on water while blowing bubbles out of his head; hang him on the cross and, well, he just hangs there looking sad and making you feel guilty. You can accessorize Babbling Jesus with such items as a crown of thorns and a seasonal wardrobe, including Ski Instructor Jesus and Surfer Dude Jesus.

4. *G. I. Job.* You're his commanding officer. Beat him, torture him, use a magnifying glass in the sun to melt his plastic body. Sure, he'll whine and moan and hurl imprecations, but in the end he keeps coming back for more!

5. *Amish Barbie.* Hedonism is over, and so is the stylin', slutty Barbie who was definitely Left Behind. But this perennial favorite is being retrofitted to jibe with the End Times. Amish Barbie is covered from head-to-toe in drab, formless skirts

and tops, and comes with an array of accessories, including buckle shoes, a buggy whip, and a butter churn. To make sure Amish Barbie doesn't get lonely or isn't stoned for being an unmarried hussy, there's also Amish Ken. Tug on his beard and he says things such as: "If you would thrive, be up by five; for there is health, and certain wealth when at the plough, or milking a cow."

END TIMES HOROSCOPES

A desire to know the future, a constant preoccupation of mankind since the dawn of history, will only increase during the End Times. They will turn to special End Times astrologers, such as Nostradamus, who in his will agreed to share with the author his predictions for the twelve signs during the End Times.

Aries: You've got a moon in Virgo, and it is plummeting toward Earth as we speak.

Taurus: You had to be stubborn and get loaded instead of going to church. Now you're not only Left Behind but on "Jesus' Most Wanted" list.

Gemini: That little devil on his shoulder will tell you to bet your life savings on a cockfight. [*Editor's Note:* One of the only sports left during the Tribulation.] Don't do it. . . . Okay, if you have to, bet the mortgage on Mister Charlie.

Cancer: Satan will ask you to buy a Lotto ticket from him. He will say, "You've got to be in it to win it" and "You never know." But you do know: The game is fixed. Everybody—winners and losers alike—goes to Hell.

Leo: You will be drafted to fight in the Lord's army, but at the physical, you will be classified 4-F and instead spend Armageddon entertaining the troops as one of the Andrews Sisters—Maxene, I think.

Virgo: You're royally screwed. That's right—you're going to be cornholed by Prince Charles.

Libra: The Antichrist will appear on a local cable broadcast in your area as a nude talk-show host. He will invite you on as a guest. Do not accept the invitation. No guest has ever returned alive.

Scorpio: Now is not a good time to adopt a pet. Especially a talking scorpion.

Sagittarius: God will lock you in a boardroom, look you in the eye, and say, "You're fired!"

Capricorn: Satan will turn you into a goat. I mean, isn't that what   you wanted all along?

Pisces: You should know better than to believe in the false idol of astrology. For that, you will spend the rest of eternity chained to Miss Cleo.

Aquarius: The End is Near. Now, don't you wish you didn't waste your life?

CHAPTER SIXTEEN

Sex and Relationships

The Rapture will have a major impact on our sexual relationships. Couples will be torn asunder as wives who assumed their marriages were rock solid will be left staring at a pile of clothes instead of husbands, and husbands who took their wives for granted will regret it when they realize they're being served divorce papers by Jesus.

In the aftermath, Oprah will write a best-selling book entitled *Left Behind and Loving It,* and Dr. Phil will counter with *Tribulation Rescue Strategies,* in which he will claim that "Armageddon is the Lord's version of tough love."

Some men will use the Rapture as an excuse to break up with a woman in whom they've lost interest. They will leave notes saying, "Darling, by the time you read this, I'll be in Heaven with Jesus" while they're actually in Atlantic City with a stripper. Rapture lonely hearts support groups will spring up, as Left Behinders bond by sharing self-pitying tales of witnessing their spouses disappear. (Some right in the middle of intercourse—a phenomenon to be known as coitus Rapturuptus.)

Experts will ponder the effect of the Rapture and the Tribulation on sexual psychology. Will women become less choosy during the end of the world? (Yes, every place but Manhattan, where the women still will think, "Sure, he's the Lord, but what's his salary?") Will they seek out men who seem strong and able to protect them against seven-headed dragons? And will men pursue any woman as long as she doesn't resemble a seven-headed dragon? (Well, this is already their MO.) And what are there new rules for post-Rapture dating? We asked Jaclyn Michaels-Skidmore, author of *The Rules of End-Times Dating*, what she envisioned:

After the Rapture, the stakes are going to be a lot higher. More women will try to date Jesus or Satan directly. Jesus, because he's their meal ticket to everlasting life, and Satan, because he's the ultimate bad boy. We recommend the following strategies:

The Rules for Dating Satan
1. Always address him as "Prince" or "Your Lordship."
2. Don't ask too many probing questions about his "career." (Trust us: you don't want to know.)
3. Let him make the first move.
4. Don't tell him he smells like fire and brimstone.

5. Don't return his phone calls; make him appear in a puff of smoke.

6. Whatever you do, don't ever sign a prenup (or any other kind of pact), even if he promises you the world.

7. If you catch him cheating on you, give him an ultimatum: it's either you or the other woman. If he threatens to turn you into a braying mule, drop the subject.

8. If God couldn't change him, what makes you think you can?

9. If he starts to lose interest, suddenly start showing up in Church—oh, does that make him jealous!

10. Remember: you are a total harlot. Be proud.

The Rules for Dating Jesus

1. Be aggressive; he wants you to make the first move to prove your faith in Him. Apparently, He's very insecure.

2. When you go on a date, let Him pay. If He tells you He's just a poor carpenter, dump Him.

3. Be patient if He stops to heal some leper during your date.

4. Stop dating Him if he doesn't give you a romantic gift on your birthday. Frankincense and myrrh don't count.

5. Dump Him if during the first two weeks he doesn't promise to absolve you of all your sins.

6. No washing his feet on the first date.

7. If He tells you He is married to the church, tell Him you don't date married men.
8. Don't tell your therapist that you're dating the Son of God.
9. If He tells you He can't make a date because He's going to be crucified, dump Him. He's a psycho.
10. It's not Him, it's you.

Signs That the Lord Just Isn't Into You

- He never answers your prayers.
- He doesn't send his Mom to appear to you like she did to that babe at Lourdes.
- You try to speak in tongues, but the best you can manage is a few tourist phrases in Swedish.
- You stay chaste and stay home, while the harlots get all the guys.
- You're Left Behind

CHAPTER SEVENTEEN

Left Behind—What to Do After God Breaks Up with You

Being Left Behind is a terrible feeling. You may lie in bed for days, hugging your ex-boyfriend's underwear (out of which he was Raptured), and watching the Oxygen channel. You may down a pint of paint thinner, rush to the nearest dive, and let yourself be picked up by a traveling fax machine salesman named Irv. You may also take your ex's underwear, that cheap perfume he regifted you for your birthday, and his K-Tel Collection, *God's Top 40,* along with some fetish objects you bought at the local Wiccan store, build a voodoo altar, and cast an evil spell on his soul. If you find yourself taking this last step, get immediate professional help. And by "professional," I mean anybody who you have to pay to give you advice.

At this point, however, the deeper reality will hit you: this is much worse than being dumped by your boyfriend. You have been rejected by the Son of God. That's deep. You will feel like Eve cast out of the Garden, or Lot's wife, or Joan Crawford in *Mildred Pierce*. (*Note:* If you feel like Hedda Lettuce doing Joan Crawford in *Mildred Pierce,* well, the Lord warned you that you shouldn't be living in Chelsea.)

However, don't despair. There are plenty of self-help books written specifically to heal the Rapture's broken hearts and help you get on with your life during the nightmare of the Tribulation.

Titles such as:

- *Smart Women, Foolish Choices (Special Rapture Edition)*. You might be a tiger in the boardroom, but when it came to choosing a mate for eternity, you went with ultimate rogue Satan over Jesus, the Son of God. Sure, Satan was the better lover (I mean, Jesus is into that whole "new virginity" thing), but now the Evil One has dumped you and Christ won't take you on the rebound. This book will allow you to identify the self-destructive patterns in your life and help you make healthier choices the next time around. If there is a next time.

- *Codependent with Jesus No More*. This classic has been adapted to help those of you who are in controlling, dysfunctional relationships with the Son of God. Here is an excerpt:

*The sun was shining. It was a beautiful day when I
met Him. Then everything went crazy.*
                    —*Mary M., involved with Jesus*

*Sleep was all I could seem to do these days. But
whenever I awoke, my first feeling was pain—pain
because of my fear that my relationship with Jesus
was over. The love was gone—extinguished by all the
healing of the lame and the raising of the dead and
the miracles and the time he spent with the fallen
women. I couldn't face the fact that He had a compulsion to "save" people. I thought I could "save"
Him. But I couldn't. I couldn't stop Him from
making crazy speeches in public that nobody could
understand. And I couldn't stop Him from
destroying Himself. Why did He need to have to
change the world? Why wasn't I enough?*

- *Don't Sweat the Small Stuff (and It's All Small
  Stuff, Except for That Giant Meteor Hurtling
  toward Your House)*

• • •

Often we allow ourselves to get all worked up over little
things that, upon closer examination, just aren't that big a
deal. Like the fact that Gog and Magog* demolished your

---

*Creatures that appear in several books of the Bible, including Genesis,
Ezekiel, and Revelation. Wikipedia says, "They are variously presented as
men, supernatural beings (giants or demons), national groups, or lands."

house as they rampaged through your city, leaving death and destruction in their wake. Rather than let it go and get on with your day, you convince yourself that you're justified in your anger. You play out an imaginary confrontation with Gog and Magog in your mind. Why not just let it go? Try to have compassion for Gog and Magog, who must be in incredible pain to have to strike out at the world like that. And imagine how painful it must've been for them to have to go through their entire lives with such ridiculous names. So many people spend so much of their life energy "sweating the small stuff" that they completely lose touch with the magic and beauty of life.

RAPTURE ADVICE FROM "SHAQUITA BANANA," GOD'S FAVORITE TRANNY

The Rapture and Tribulation world will be unlike anything any of us has ever seen. Every aspect of our lives will be irrevocably altered. The old rules will go out the window. You'll need a guide, a seer, someone to steer you through the Tribulation's shoals and answer the many questions that you undoubtedly will have. Someone who is tight with the Lord and who also looks great in a Bob Mackey rhinestone number. That would be Shaquita Banana, who here shares some of the many solicitations she has received:

Q: Is it possible to have sex during the Rapture?

A: You better believe it, babe, but since it will take place "in the twinkling of an eye," it will have to be a quickie. And both of you will be on top.

Q: What if I plan a big dinner party and the day

before the party several of my guests are Raptured? What should I tell the caterer?

A: Just say there's been a change of plans and you'll need less potato salad.

Q: All of the cool kids were Raptured and I was Left Behind. I'm so embarrassed! Now I'm stuck with a bunch of dorks who spend all their time playing in Middle Earth and watching DVDs of *Dr. Who*. What should I do?

A: Work hard and maybe you'll be taken up by Jesus at the Last Judgment. Then you can strut into Heaven like Miss Thing and you'll be, like, stylin' and you tell those cool kids "In your face, bitches!"

Q: Ever since the Rapture, my satellite TV reception has sucked. Who can I sue?

A: Shaquita has had a lot of complaints from people about satellite TV, cell-phone reception, and Internet connections. Some attorneys are smelling a payday and starting humongous class-action suits. The Lord could never afford to pay off all these people, so he panicked and fled the country. Last I heard, he was living in Argentina.

Q: Here's an SAT question: If Suzie was Raptured in one-eighteenth of a second and Heaven is 3,228,000 miles from Earth, how fast was Suzie going?

A: How the hell should Shaquita know, babe? Shaquita got kicked out of high school for giving the gym teacher a "banana split."

CHAPTER EIGHTEEN
....

Left Behind and Begrudging It (PTRSD—Posttraumatic Rapture Stress Disorder and Other Tribulations)

Feeling the cosmic rejection of the Lord after being Left Behind isn't the only psychological disorder that will afflict people still on Earth. Many people will suffer from PTRSD— Posttraumatic Rapture Stress Disorder.

WHAT IS POSTTRAUMATIC RAPTURE STRESS DISORDER?
Posttraumatic Rapture Stress Disorder, or PTRSD, is a psychiatric disorder that can occur following the experience of witnessing a family member, friend, or anybody, really, suddenly bolting into the sky and disappearing into space.

Most Rapture survivors return to normal given a little time. However, some people will have stress reactions that do not go away on their own, or may even get worse over time. These individuals may develop PTRSD. People who suffer from PTRSD often relive the Rapture through nightmares, flashbacks, and bad novels; have difficulty sleeping; and feel detached, ashamed, and guilt-ridden. They may also feel as if they're losing touch with reality.

PTRSD victims may also suffer from a compulsion to try to Rapture themselves so they can rejoin their loved ones. They may climb to the top of tall buildings, bridges, cliffs, and other heights and attempt to jump off, while screaming, "Catch me, Jesus!" This is clearly an irrational act, as Jesus has never caught anybody. (One cynical entrepreneur has tried to take advantage of these deluded souls by selling them "Rapture-chutes" that will allow them to "float gracefully up to Heaven.")

PTRSD is marked by clear psychological symptoms: depression, anxiety, and even multiple personality disorder, in which the afflicted person comes to believe that he or she sometimes is Paris Hilton and other times is Perez Hilton.

PTRSD is complicated by the fact that it frequently occurs in conjunction with related disorders such as substance abuse, memory loss, and PTTSD (Pre-Tribulation Traumatic Stress Disorder). The disorder is also associated with impairment of the afflicted person's ability to function in social or family life, and may manifest itself in occupational instability, marital problems, and a strange compulsion to have their hamster placed in a gated hamster community.

OTHER PSYCHIC DISTURBANCES

The DSM-IV will have to be drastically expanded during the Tribulation. In fact, the American Psychiatric Association will have to compile a DSM-V just to include all the strange new psychic disturbances caused by the trauma of the End Times. The most prevalent will be Left Behind Syndrome, the sufferers of which feel that they are "victims" of a "patriarchal God" and that, therefore, society owes them restitution. However, since during the Tribulation there will hardly be any society left, their pleas will fall upon deaf ears. There also will be many cases of:

RECOVERED MEMORIES OF SATANIC RITUAL ABUSE

In the past, the testimony of children who supposedly "recovered" memories of Satanic ritual abuse with the help of psychotherapists was considered suspect. (After all, since when did psychotherapists ever help anyone?) Despite hundreds of thousands of reported cases, nobody could prove there were Satanic cults kidnapping children and forcing them to participate in horrifying rituals.

But after the Rapture and during the Tribulation, Satan himself will actually kidnap children by luring them into the woods with an offer of Lick Your Wounds Candy Scabs* and then society will realize, "We should've listened to those wacky kids and their paranoid parents, after all!"

Here is one victim's shocking testimony: "I was eight years old. I'm an only child, and both of my parents were Raptured. I was home alone in the house. After I got over the shock of losing my parents, I had trouble sleeping, so I stayed up all night watching TV. One night I was watching TV and there was an infomercial for something called the George Foreman

*An actual candy.

Human-Sized Grill. I thought that was really creepy. Then, suddenly, the face of Satan took over the screen. He told me to meet him at Taco Bell. I was terrified, but I couldn't seem to resist him. So I got on my bike and rode to Taco Bell, in the minimall. When I got there, the place was packed with customers, mostly kids but some grown-ups. Satan was there, wearing a white apron and a chef's hat. I couldn't believe it! Satan—the night manager at Taco Bell!

"He told me to put on an apron and took me back to the kitchen. There were piles of stuff. Taco shells, refried beans, plastic-looking cheese, and a pile of some sort of animal parts. I asked Satan what it was and he said, "Don't worry. It's all chicken." There were also stacks of scallions and a barrel of scummy-looking water with a sign on it that said, 'E. coli.' He pointed to the scallions and said, 'Chop those scallions, dip them in the barrel, and then put them in the tacos.'

"So I did what he told me. We sold a lot of tacos that night. But people were, like, doubling over and clutching their stomachs, vomiting blood in the parking lot, and just, like, passing out.

"After we closed for the night, Satan brought out a couple of cases of Bud and we got trashed. One kid got so sloshed, he fell into the barrel. First his face turned blue, then he started to choke and throw up and in a minute or so he was dead. Then—and this is hard for me to even say— Satan made us chop him up and throw him in the pile of 'chicken.' When we were finished, he said, 'You are now my children. You will do as I say, and in return I will pay you $5.75 an hour without benefits.' I asked him, 'Isn't it wrong to chop up a human corpse and put the parts in chicken tacos and then sell the tacos to people?' He stared at me with his red eyes glowing like hot bricks and said, 'Think outside the bun.'

"Well, I stayed at the Taco Bell for a couple of weeks, but one night, when Satan's back was turned, I snuck out the side entrance, got on my bike and rode and rode until I couldn't ride any more and was starving. So I stopped at a Taco Bell. And here I am. . . . Oh, I ordered the 'chicken' chalupas."

Rebuttal from a Taco Bell Spokesperson
We must protest the foregoing incident, which we feel is inauthentic, inaccurate, and libelous, for the following reasons:

1. We have never employed anybody named Satan. Taco Bell takes pride in our workforce and selects each employee on the basis of rigorous criteria, including physical health, mental acuity, moral rectitude, and the absence of little red horns.
2. The *E. coli* scallions could not have been added to the tacos at a local branch of our chain. The *E. coli* is added at our central taco-processing plant in the Dominican Republic.

RECOVERED MEMORIES OF SATANIC ABUSE: CASE #2
"Hi, my name is Rosemary. I'm thirty-three years old and a legal assistant. One night I was at a club with my girlfriends and this hot-looking older guy started chatting me up. Goatee. Nice suit. He had a red tail, but what can I say? I was drunk. And my parents were always telling me I was too picky about men. He noticed me staring at the tail, and he said,

'Birth defect. Don't worry. I'm used to it.' Then he pointed to the ground and instead of feet, he had hooves. I was freaked out and got really nervous, and I just blurted out, 'Wow, you must have a hard time shopping for shoes.' I know—stupid. But he was cool. Nonjudgmental. Said he was in the human-potential movement and that he had a kind of organization, like EST, only eviler. I laughed—I guess I've always liked bad boys. I asked him if he was married and he said, 'No. I came close once or twice, but the tail was a deal-breaker.' It sounds stupid now, but I felt sorry for the guy. And I gotta admit: He was different from all the account execs and shoe salesmen that usually hit on me.

"He bought us a bottle of Courvoisier and, well, one thing led to another—my biological clock ticking was part of it—and I went home with him that night. He had a condo in a pretty remote area in the woods near a golf course.

"When we got there, he took me into the outdoor Jacuzzi and there's, like, fifteen other women in there. I thought, 'Oh, no, this guy's a freakin' Mormon.' But he must've seen the surprised look on my face, and he said, 'Yeah, I know it looks weird. But it's cool. We're all one big happy family.' Anyway, the sex was amazing. I mean, if you've never done it with a half-man-half-goat, you don't know what you're missing. So I moved in.

"At first he said that he would take care of me, I could quit my job, blah, blah, blah. So I did. But after a month or so he started dropping hints that he was in a 'financial bind.' It had to do with the IRS not allowing him tax-free status or something.

"He told me I had to find a job and help 'pitch in' around the 'complex.' At first, he suggested I work at a local Taco

Bell that he had some kind of interest in. But the board of health closed it down after a bunch of customers, well, died.

"Then one day he cornered me and said, 'Why don't we have a baby?' He knew my weakness: I'd always wanted a child. But I was afraid that the kid might be born with a tail and hooves, which, I mean, forget about getting into a good preschool. But he said he had a test and everything was cool.

"Still, I was suspicious. And then one day one of the other wives took me to this secret dungeon where the 'children' were. They were all his kids by the other wives, and I mean it was like a real freak show. There was a boy with two mouths, who kept saying when he grew up he wanted to be a congressman. And another who had the body of a donkey and the head of Howie Mandel. It was . . . horrible. I dashed out the back entrance and he didn't see me, but just as I was leaving, I saw Donald Rumsfeld get out of a limo and go inside. . . ."

CHAPTER NINETEEN

The Post-Trib: What Happens After the End of the World?

Okay, God has vanquished Satan and the forces of evil, the souls of the just have been resurrected, and history is, well, history.

Now what? Well, we know that God and his chosen will idle away the rest of eternity spooning up ambrosia and listening to Heavenly Muzak. Eternal life? BOR-ING!

But what about Satan and Jesus? The way I see it, there are three possibilities for Satan: (1) God kills him; (2) He repents and God takes him back into the fold; or, most likely, (3) God punishes him by forcing to star in a sitcom that's televised only in Heaven via closed-circuit TV.

DEVIL MAY CARE

OPEN on suburban living room, only looking like a grade 5
hurricane had just swept through it: furniture in tatters,
garbage strewn on the floor, chunks of plaster hanging from
the ceiling, and so on. MRS. SATAN and her children, JASON
and BRITNEY, all in fire-engine red devil suits. The kids are
studiously doing homework.

MRS. SATAN

Come on, kids, stop fooling around with that homework.
Time to hit the video games.

BRITNEY

Oh, mom!!!

JASON

Do we have to?

MRS. SATAN

It's either that—or watch porn videos.

BRITNEY

Some choice . . .

JASON

Mom, if I win at *Grand Theft Auto,* can I go to algebra
camp this summer?

MRS. SATAN

Absolutely not.

JASON

But why not? Billy and Freddy Pomeroy's parents are letting
them go.

MRS. SATAN

The Pomeroys are Christians. And I told you to stay away
from them. They're a bad influence.

(Enter SATAN, *in a fire-engine red business suit, his tail dis-
creetly hanging out the back. Canned applause, which Satan
seems to acknowledge.)*

SATAN

Honey, I'm home!

He trips and does a full gainer on an algebra book one of his
kids has left on the floor. Laugh track howls.

SATAN

Ouch! What did I tell you kids about leaving your algebra
books on the floor?

MRS. SATAN

Not only that—they won't play their video games or watch
porn. And you should see their report cards. Straight A's.
And perfect marks for behavior.

SATAN

(to JASON, BRITNEY*)*

Is that why I work and slave all day? Just today I started a war and two civil insurrections and crashed a jetliner in Brazil, killing all 216 people on board. And after all that, the least I expect is to see my children following in my evil footsteps. But nooooooooooo!

MRS. SATAN
(*to* SATAN)
It's your fault. You're too easy on them.

SATAN
Hey, you're the one raising them. (*mimicking Freddy Prinze in* Chico and the Man) Ees not my job.

MRS. SATAN
You—and those Pomeroys. Those holier-than-thou creeps are poisoning our kids' minds with their Jesus talk. That Molly Pomeroy won't be satisfied until she's martyred.

(Doorbell rings.)

MRS. SATAN
Who could that be?

SATAN
Uh-oh . . .

MRS. SATAN
What?

SATAN
I . . . invited the Pomeroys over for dinner.

MRS. SATAN
You WHAT?

SATAN
Herb's been bugging me for months to invite them over. I
said "Fuck you, you self-righteous asshole" a million times,
but he just won't get the message.

MRS. SATAN
I don't understand you! You're supposed to be the Prince of
Darkness. But you're just a big a pushover!

(Doorbell rings.)

MRS. SATAN
I'm not letting them in.

SATAN
Wait! I've got an idea!

MRS. SATAN
Oh, great! Einstein's got another brainstorm. Like crucifying
Jesus to stamp out Christianity! That really worked out,
didn't it?

(Boffo canned laughs.)

SATAN
I'll stall them while you go in and poison the meatloaf. Then
it's *bon appetito*—and *finito!*

MRS. SATAN

You want me to ruin a perfectly good meatloaf I spent all
day on!

SATAN

Please! I'll take you to T. J. Maxx and you can watch women
maul each other to death over a Prada sale.

MRS. SATAN

Ah! You know my weakness.

(She goes into the kitchen. SATAN *opens the front door.)*

SATAN

Herb! Dotty! Come on in!

(Enter HERB *and* DOTTY, middle-aged, white, dorkily
dressed, HERB *in a Western shirt, bolo tie, and extra-large
comfort-fit jeans, and* DOTTY *in a long, peasant skirt, old
pedal pushers, and a bonnet. She holds a covered dish.)*

HERB

Thanks!

(They enter the living room.)

DOTTY

Why, your home is so, homey!

SATAN

Thanks.

HERB

Where's the wife?

SATAN

Oh, she's in the kitchen putting the finishing touch on a meatloaf.

DOTTY

Oh, my, she shouldn't have! You see, I brought a meatloaf!

She hands him her dish, a meatloaf.

SATAN

Er, thanks . . .

(Enter MRS. SATAN, carrying her meatloaf.)

MRS. SATAN

Oh, hello, Herb, Dotty. Dinner is served.

SATAN

Guess what, dear? Dotty brought her own meatloaf . . .

[There follows an elaborate bit of physical comedy in which the poison meatloaf and the nonpoison meatloaf get switched around, Satan and Mrs. Satan end up eating the poison meatloaf and the Pomeroys eat the nontoxic one before finally leaving. I know, it's not exactly *Seinfeld,* but trust me: in Heaven—the Nielsen's? Through the roof.]

• • •

As for Jesus, we have a scoop: He's not going back to Heaven. Now that he's got a taste of the limelight, he's decided to try his hand at acting, too. And right off the bat, He will land a movie role, as the star of a romantic comedy called *Prodigal Son* for Universal Pictures. According to *Variety,** a writer named Gigi Levangie Grazer will receive a six-figure deal just for the concept. "It's a love it or hate it idea, but we're not aiming to offend," she says. "He won't be having sex. It'll be a disarming romantic comedy, a story of unrequited love, sort of like *Splash*."

The story is about a workaholic single mom in L.A. who gets fixed up by her mother, and her date winds up being Jesus Christ. You see, the good-looking, sweet-natured carpenter has returned for Armageddon and earns some extra cash working at Ikea.

For that alone, he deserves to be crucified.

*Actual story in December 8, 2006, issue of *Variety*.

CHAPTER TWENTY

God: The Last Word

First of all, I want to give a shout-out to my homie, Jim Gerard.

Great read.

Moving along, I bet you want to know about . . . how should I put it? . . . My future plans. Especially those regarding you. It's always all about you, isn't it?

First, there is no Rapture. That's right—you heard me. I mean, did you really expect me to summon 144,000 of you at once? And to disappear you out of your clothes? Do I look like David Copperfield?

I don't do magic.

And that whole bit about me empowering Satan and then

spending seven years fighting him on Earth. . . . Like I need that mishigas? I don't have enough to do? You believe that, you're spending too much time playing Dungeons & Dragons.

Besides, I got no beef with Satan. He does his thing; I do mine.

Now let me get to the most important part of this message. I've heard a lot of complaints over the years from you people who think I'm aloof, who wonder why I haven't revealed myself more obviously (what do you expect me to do, go on *The View*?), why I don't respond to your prayers, and why I "allow" all kinds of tragic mayhem—like six-year-olds being gang-raped in Africa, to name one story I just happened to catch on the news—to happen.

I'll tell you why I don't reveal myself to you.

I'm too embarrassed to show my face!

Ever since the beginning, all you people have ever done is fight each other, connive for power, lie, rob, cheat, and engage in mass murder. You turn the page on genocide, yet hyperventilate if someone parks in your space. Rather than live with tolerance and acceptance of others, you can't wait to discriminate against anyone who doesn't look, act, or think exactly the same as you. The things you do—I spend entire days kneeling over the toilet. Do you know how bad you have to be to make God puke?

And you do it all in my name. That's the part that hurts.

When I gave you free will, I thought you would be grateful. After all, I could've created a race of yes men. But the only time you've used that free will was to do unspeakable things. And most of you didn't want any part of it in the first place.

You couldn't wait to give away your power to the first bully, tyrant, or infomercial pitchman who came along.

I thought I knew evil. But some of you—I won't name names . . . Hitler . . . Stalin . . . Bush, the whole family . . . they make Adam, Eve, and Cain look like pikers.

Ultimately, it's my bad. I created you in my image. If that's how I appear to you, well, I've got to look in the mirror.

Even now, I'm sure you're not listening. You're too preoccupied with your own salvation. You're dying to know: who gets saved and who's Left Behind? Well, let me tell you: it's a crapshoot.

After all, who am I to judge?

Advance Praise for
Beam Me Up, Jesus

"*Beam Me Up, Jesus* . . . the title alone gives me a headache."

—Pope Benedict XVI

"Somebody ought to take out this guy."

—Pat Robertson

"The zinfandel-swilling, moral relativist child molester who wrote this is aiding and abetting America's enemies, and he should pay!"

—Bill O'Reilly

"Jim Gerard is laughing now . . . but he won't be laughing when he finds himself doing the backstroke in a river of hot, molten lava for the rest of eternity."

　　　　　　　　　　　　　—James Dobson, Focus on the Family

"[Gerard] has declared war on the Rapture. He must be stopped. Jesus, are you listening?"

　　　　　　　　　—Donald Wildmon, American Family Association

Acknowledgments

I would like to thank my representatives at Imprint Agency, Stephany Evans and Gary Heidt, for their encouragement and support (without Stephany, this book would not exist); my simpatico editor, Carl Bromley; Michael Santamaria, who reviewed the manuscript with a discerning theological (and comedic) eye; Richard Lally, for many years of editorial and personal guidance; Dr. Stephen DeFronzo, my "manager," for his steadfast confidence in me (keep pitching, Doc!); Jamie Larowitz and Steve Sherman, for their generosity and friendship; my dear friends Emmett McConnell and Jodie Moore; my brother Joseph Gerard; Henry Gerard, a locomotive-phile and my favorite walking companion; Mr. Richard Sonoda, that kindest and wisest of men, and Sam Pedalino, for his longtime support.

Most of all I would like to thank Marion Gerard, for her love and devotion (and for sending me to Catholic school—that peerless incubator of atheists), and the late Peter Pedalino, a secular saint who inculcated in me a love of learning and a healthy distrust of officialdom, and from whom I inherited a gift for beholding with sardonic wonder the follies of man.